MONASTIC WISDOM SERIES

Agnes Day, ocso

Light in the Shoe Shop

A Cobbler's Contemplations

MONASTIC WISDOM SERIES: NUMBER THIRTY-SIX

Light in the Shoe Shop

A Cobbler's Contemplations

by

Agnes Day, OCSO

α

Cistercian Publications
www.cistercianpublications.org

LITURGICAL PRESS
Collegeville, Minnesota
www.litpress.org

A Cistercian Publications title published by Liturgical Press

Cistercian Publications
Editorial Offices
Abbey of Gethsemani
3642 Monks Road
Trappist, Kentucky 40051
www.cistercianpublications.org

© 2013 by Order of Saint Benedict, Collegeville, Minnesota. All rights reserved. No part of this book may be reproduced in any form, by print, microfilm, micro- fiche, mechanical recording, photocopying, translation, or by any other means, known or yet unknown, for any purpose except brief quotations in reviews, without the previous written permission of Liturgical Press, Saint John's Abbey, PO Box 7500, Collegeville, Minnesota 56321-7500. Printed in the United States of America.

1   2   3   4   5   6   7   8   9

Library of Congress Cataloging-in-Publication Data

Day, Agnes, 1933–
    Light in the shoe shop : a cobbler's contemplations / by Agnes Day, OCSO.
        p.   cm. — (Monastic wisdom series ; no. 36)
    ISBN 978-0-87907-036-6 — ISBN 978-0-87907-763-1 (e-book)
    1. Day, Agnes, 1933–   2. Cistercian nuns—Massachusetts—Wrentham
(Town)—Spiritual life.   3. Monastic and religious life of women—
Massachusetts—Wrentham (Town)   4. Shoemakers—Religious life.   I. Title.

BX4705.D2825A3   2013
271'.97—dc23

[B]   2012043965

The Lord has become like me,
   in order that I might receive Him;
He was reckoned like myself,
   in order that I might put Him on;
And I trembled not when I saw Him,
   because He was gracious to me;
Like my nature He became
   that I might learn from Him,
And like my form,
   that I might not turn back from Him.

The Father has given the word of knowledge
   to be seen by those who belong to Him,
That they may recognize who made them,
   and not suppose that they came of themselves;
For knowledge He has appointed as His way,
   He has widened and extended it;
He has brought it to all perfection,
   and has set over it the footprints of His light;
And I walked therein
   from the beginning to the end.
For by Him was the path of knowledge made,
   and it rested in the Son.

The Odes of Solomon (AD 100–150), Ode VII
tr. J. Rendel Harris

*To my dearly loved community of
Mount Saint Mary's Abbey, Wrentham,
whose story underlies this book*

CONTENTS

FOREWORD

You will scarcely ever come across a quieter yet more intensely glowing book than the one you are now holding. The words *precious*, *gentle*, and *wise* have been used by reviewers to describe its style and contents. From my editorial familiarity with our other volumes I would like to add a fourth qualifier: *unique*. Seldom will a reader be afforded a more intimate glance into the day-to-day experience of living the cloistered life in feminine mode than can be had from these pages. But, beyond the specificity of the monastic context, I can equally say that seldom will a reader be afforded a more intimate glance quite simply into the way a generous and listening heart comes to perceive the world after being schooled by all the joys and many sorrows of self-surrender.

This book is decidedly not just one more item in the picturesque genre of the "nun's story." Rather, for all its slenderness, the volume bears a strong witness to the fact that a human life that stakes its all on loving will gradually become transfused with light.

Take the book off to some quiet corner and, if you allow the elemental words it offers to wash over you slowly, I suspect you will gain far more than simply a satisfied curiosity concerning the exterior details of life in the cloister. Indeed, the gentle and luminous sensibility of every sentence is apt to imbue the receptive reader with a gladness and a serenity that will at first be hard to account for. You will find yourself spontaneously smiling; your eyes may even begin shedding certain scales you didn't know were obstructing your vision. Only slowly will the awareness emerge that the author has somehow managed to pass on to you, in nuanced yet utterly down-to-earth language, something of the interior spiritual fruits of the life she herself has long lived on a daily basis.

In her "cobbler's contemplations"—no metaphor here: the author did indeed make belts and mend her sisters' shoes for some years—Mother Agnes reveals the very simple secret of monastic life, a secret she shows to be an inseparable combination of mindfulness and fidelity: continual *mindfulness* of God's transformative presence and action and, in response, equally continual *fidelity* to each of the minutely detailed ways in which that loving divine presence woos the contemplative's heart. And let us never forget that contemplatives do not dwell only in literal cloisters.

Whether the author is musing on the precise angle at which a ray of light enters her shoe shop, or pondering the specific solution to a sister's torn sandals, or wondering at the way a new season of the year is infiltrating the Wrentham countryside, we sense that Mother Agnes' spirit holds out every moment of her Cistercian life like a bucket in which to catch the healing rain of grace. From her experience we ourselves slowly learn that, to the contemplative soul, *God is to be found in the details*, and this fundamental truth accounts for the fact that, as we read these pages, we find it impossible to separate spiritual from physical, this-worldly from other-worldly. To the heart that strives to pray always, eternity has already invaded time.

Poetry has always been the privileged form for expressing the inexpressible, and so it is fitting to append a small selection of Agnes Day's poems to her shoe shop meditations and her autobiographical sketch. In this way the volume will in the end leave us suspended in a resonant silence—the very silence of God's love, that is forever "widening us in the torrent" as it seeks its way through us to all others. I tend to think that whisking us off to this plane of experience was the one motivation that persuaded such a self-effacing person to agree to the publication of rather personal material. But she speaks for herself on this subject in her preface.

I am particularly grateful to Mother Agnes for agreeing to write a retrospective of her life before entering the monastery. For surely many will want to relate, with great spiritual profit, the young girl growing up on two continents and the dedicated college student to the mature nun who confined her interior illuminations to paper and eventually accepted the enormous task of being the abbess of a large community. In the end, however, perhaps the greatest lesson Mother Agnes Day unconsciously teaches us is the intense glee with which she has gratefully returned to being, quite simply, Sister Agnes, just another member of the faithful Wrentham sisterhood.

Simeon Leiva, OCSO

PREFACE

In the Beginning . . .

First, some explanation is needed at the beginning of this little book. The bulk of it was originally written a few years before I was elected abbess. It came into being as an answer to a frequent question from people interested in our life as Cistercian Nuns. The question would follow my attempts to suggest books on our vocation, all by male authors. The person interrogating me would then say: "But isn't there something written by Cistercian women?" At that time there wasn't much written in our native language by the nuns, and what little there was could not be easily obtained. I decided to write something myself, for that purpose. I did so, and gave it to our abbess, Mother Angela Norton, for her approbation. She was already quite ill, but she read the manuscript and returned it to me with a very positive answer. But then her illness grew quickly, making it difficult for her to take care of all the details of her community service. I was second superior at the time, and it began to take all my time and energy. Mother Angela died in January 1986. She had been abbess for 34 years. An election for her successor was held March 21, and I found myself in that new role. We are a fairly large community, and I had my hands, head, and heart full trying to fulfill the graced but difficult task, one day at a time.

I did think of the little manuscript once or twice, but felt it wasn't the time for me to do anything about publishing it. About 20 years later, in a conversation with one of my sisters, she said I should write a book. Laughing, I said I did write one, but never did anything about it. She asked to borrow the manuscript to read, and I got the notebook down from a dusty upper shelf and

gave it to her. A few days later she came back to me with enthu-
siasm and encouraged me to publish it. After we talked a little I
decided to try it on the community as our reading at the main
meal of the day. That was done, and the response was most encouraging; but I put off doing anything about it because I still
had all I could manage in order to do my best as abbess. I retired
after 22 years of abbatial service in May 2008, and thought of the
manuscript, but presumed it was now too old.

I was asked to be one of two presenters for the yearly seminar held in one of our monasteries each year for the "juniors"
(those with temporary vows) of all the Cistercian (OCSO) monasteries in the USA, both monks and nuns. The invitation was
for May 2010. The seminar for that year was to be held in the
monastery of Gethsemani in Kentucky. After long struggles to
produce ten talks, leading me almost to give up in discourage-
ment and resign from the job, I thought of the little manuscript.
I got it out and read it over, realizing that it said just what I
wanted to share with the juniors: to find the Extraordinary within
the Ordinary, as I had titled my theme. To make a long story
short, I did that, and it was received and responded to so well
that I could not mistake the Lord's work in the process.

It seems the material isn't too old after all, and could even
be welcomed by people in different walks of life. Of course, many
things have changed since this book was first conceived, for example the two sisters' graves we had then in our cemetery have
multiplied to eighteen; our liturgy now is almost entirely in En-
glish; the cows are gone and we now have a small herd of sheep,
watched over by a llama and one or sometimes two devoted
sisters; we built an infirmary wing and library and had a complete renovation of our church; among other things. . . . But the
heart of the life we live together remains the same, and we can
still identify with what was written so long ago.

Agnes Day, OCSO

I

LUMINOUS DARKNESS

(May)

Every day has a quiet beginning here in the Abbey. It is fitting, then, that this reflection of one person's monastic experience should begin quietly too, in the silence of the hour before dawn.

The Office of Vigils is over, and the stars are paler than they were at 3 AM, but the birds are still asleep. I half kneel, half sit on my prayer bench in the dark church, held in that mysterious name of the Lord: I am He who is always with you. There are a few small noises that indicate I am not alone, and yet I am solitary because of the dark, because no one sees my face but God.

The sanctuary lamp sends a delicate, wavering fan of light up the wall to pool on the ceiling—an illumination so subtle it will soon be lost in the gray light of dawn. It wakes one small gleam from the tabernacle, and half reveals the statue of our Lady fixed on the wall above it. The paschal candle is only a black silhouette. No flame crowns it. It is extinguished because Jesus has ascended to the Father; and yet the sanctuary lamp makes its gentle statement: He is with us. He is with us to the end of the world. It is not a contradiction. Really there is no now or then, no here or there in this matter of presence.

The dark has a message too. I cannot see clearly, but to be near God is my happiness. It is a matter of faith, not vision; love, not comprehension. Even if I am a beast before Him* with nothing to say, still I am always with Him.

---

* Psalm 72:22; *The Grail Psalter*.

1

But it is no longer so dark. The windows glow mother-of-pearl. The first sleepy robin clears his throat. I go to the scriptorium. I open the Bible on my desk, choosing Psalm 139 for my *lectio*. The first clear bird calls come through the slightly open windows, with a current of fresh air.

"O Lord, You have probed me and know me . . ." You are He who is always with me. No moment of my life, no thought, no deed of mine is hidden from You. You know me . . . (and even so, You love me)! You are closer to me than my own thoughts. I don't have to struggle to say magnificent things to You. You know my thoughts before they bubble up into consciousness, long before they have put on words. This is very comforting, but also terrifying. Sometimes You are too close because I am too afraid. "Behind me and before, You hem me in and rest Your hand on me." It's not just that my thoughts aren't always good or innocent; it's the full weight of Your holiness that is frightening. Is there no place I can hide to catch my breath? No place. There is no getting away from You. Sometimes I could cry out, You expect too much! But I know it's not so. You know, and if You ask something, it's because You give me the potential to give it, though not without straining and growing, not without a little dying.

You are with me, in me, and if I am, it is only in You. In the closeness of this relationship, what is east or west, up or down, day or night? But I do not want to hide from You. I want to be completely open, utterly known, and I want to know You even if Your glory burns me to a cinder. But this is why Jesus came—to make You known, gently, without the crushing weight of Your glory—to reveal Your love that reaches from end to end, mightily and sweetly.

All my history lies before You, from the moment I began to be to the last breath I will draw. No matter how confused and pathless life may seem, no matter my mistakes, my wrong choices, my sins, Your designs are not ruined. They are larger than that. They are as large as Your love. . . .

Even if my life should lie in ruins around me, broken in a night of sorrow, I will still believe You are with me, I will still believe in Your love. As the sun is not snuffed out by the night, but merely hidden by the bulk of earth, so would that night be.

You would spring again like the sunrise behind my shards, revealing in them a new pattern I can't begin to imagine, a design which was Your intention from all eternity.

But now I cannot think of night. The dawn is streaming in the windows. The birds are in full orchestra as the edge of the huge orange sun burns over the horizon. My eyes are no longer on the sacred text, but on the glory of the sky behind the newly leafed trees. The dawn air, sweet and dewy, flows gently across the quiet room. In my heart, a song begins—Sr. Edith's *Alleluia*. All three parts can sing in this inner choir. The music is like an Easter sunrise, like an Ascension. One ray, then two, then three, then the glad edge of the sun itself. The sun breaks free of the earth and mounts the heavens—serene, majestic.

II

THOUGHTS OF HIS HEART

(June)

Two o'clock in the afternoon. The road to the barn reflects the June heat. I've got a load of boots and shoes in the metal basket I carry, turned in for repair by some of my steady customers, my fifty-seven sisters. Fifty-eight pairs of active feet keep me busy—in fact, I never catch up. That's why nearly every afternoon finds me walking along this road, summer and winter, in fair or foul weather. Today is very fair. The mock orange is out, and its fragrance—made sharper by the sun—drifts across the road. I swing around the end of the forsythia hedge, and my destination is in full view.

The shop's building is old. It contains a printing shop at one end, a carpenter shop in the middle, and a shoe repair shop at the other end. Its walls abhor the rigidity of right angles. Daisies grow in front of the shoe shop end. It's not exactly the place to grow flowers, but that's where they grew, and who am I to make objections to self-sufficient flowers which I did not have to plant, and do not have to care for, but may simply enjoy? I scan the grass to be sure that the large milk snake that lives under the building is not out to enjoy the hot sun. Happily, it is not in sight today. Even though it is harmless (and even beneficial because it lives on small rodents), I am not comfortable with a snake! Having duly admired the daisies, I step over them and open the door.

The shoe shop is a large room, full of machinery, supplies, boots and shoes. There are cubbies full of soles and drawers full of heels, jars and bottles of nails and glue, pieces of leather and salvaged bits of old shoes, not to mention a grand assortment of special shoe repair tools. A funny-looking crucifix hangs on one wall (askew, of course, to match the wall) with a little statue of our Lady underneath it. There's no clock. Time goes into limbo in the shoe shop, so I have no need of clock or watch. Besides, the barn bell will warn me when it's time to wind up the afternoon's work. The afternoon will fly, I know. It's not just that there's a lot to do, but that I'm happy here doing it. Extending the life of footgear beyond anything the manufacturer dreamed possible is satisfying, although my sometimes unorthodox repairs would turn a real cobbler apoplectic. But my contentment has a deeper cause than that. The why of it has more to do with the why of my Cistercian monastic life, and that's not a why but a Who. Contentment is a wrong word, too. It sounds too placid for a life of exploration of the Lord's love, in which each discovery is a shock of joy.

It was a June day like this one when I came to the Abbey to enter, only hotter. The roses were out in profusion all along somebody's roadside stone wall as we drove the last couple of miles from the center of the town of Wrentham. It was the day before the Feast of the Sacred Heart. Devotion to the Sacred Heart was one of those "born Catholic" things I hadn't quite absorbed. It still felt alien to a convert of three and a half years. But then, everything else seemed strange to me too, especially the step I was taking that day. When the idea of becoming a nun first began whispering at the back of my mind, I couldn't take it seriously. "Who, *me*? Be a *nun*?" It just had to be a crazy idea of my own. But the Lord had me cornered, and when I stopped my wild thrashing, it became quite clear to me that He *was* inviting me, and of course, my answer was "yes"—wide-eyed, shaking with joy. With the inscrutable plans of His Heart, He cut right across the future I had envisioned for myself.

God is the incalculable, the uncontrollable. He just won't fit neatly into anybody's plans, play a role assigned to Him, or even let us get any clear idea of the role He is going to play. As a matter of fact, He doesn't play roles at all. *He is*, in a sense that everything and everybody else isn't. The only thing He lets us know unmistakably is that He loves us. His love is specific, individual, and very much bigger than we are. If everything else I think I know should prove false, this one fact of God's love would remain unshaken, for I know it more certainly than I know I exist.

I smile now, glancing down at my well-worn work boots and remembering my dainty black Capezios of that long-ago June day. Many a step has been taken between that day and this. My mother abbess helped me to understand that devotion to the Sacred Heart isn't just another devotion, but the most central reality in life, for it is response to God's love, made manifest in Jesus. That made all the difference. Now I'm on to Him. I know He's going to surprise me every day—Him and His joy.

Seeds of wonder, ready to sprout, are my Lord's specialties. There might be one hidden in even so prosaic a place as among the several half-finished boot repairs lined up on the table. The only rule of the game, though, is not to anticipate, since preconceptions block awareness, so I'll just get to work. Boot repairs aren't as easy or as much fun to do as shoe renovations, but they're always being needed around here. The cow barn work in particular takes its toll of rubber soles and boot leather, with work maintaining the grounds and garden coming next in wear and tear. The barn assignment is good work—close to nature and productive of wholesome food for the maintenance of life. Saint Benedict knew what he was about when he advocated manual work for his monks. It is cleansing and freeing to work hard with one's hands and whole body, especially in the type of work that is close to life—to animals and crops and the ordinary needs of human existence. Serving is one of our deepest needs, and this is a way to serve, to share in Christ's serving of others.

I started these boots yesterday. Glue alone won't hold the new soles, but hand stitching will, for a good long time. A fly buzzes against the window, and a barn cat stops to look in my open door as I stitch. My mind is free—satisfied on one level with the rhythmical placing of stitch after stitch in a strong white row, but not burdened by such a simple task. Though I am alone here, a hundred yards away my sisters are working in the barn, feeding and milking the cows, and freshening their bedding. If someone is in the carpenter shop working, I can't hear her, nor can I hear Sr. Andrée and Sr. Francis at the presses in the print shop. There are sisters making and packing candy in another building, and just beyond is our enormous vegetable garden, where Sr. Magdalen is running the rototiller and two or three others are thinning and weeding.

Our work—each at her assigned task—serves the dual purpose of self-support and spiritual health. It is work that is at the same time sabbath, because it does not take us from that basic resting in God which His love teaches us in *lectio* and prayer. Sabbath is not just our rest but an entering into God's rest, the seventh day, the Promised Land. It is an admiration of all God has done—for it is indeed good. This fundamental attitude need not be forsaken during activity. In fact, there's nothing that unties inner knots quite so well as some good work, and prayer flows more easily again after sweat. It is a healthy psychological balance to an intense inner life of prayer, keeping our feet on the ground. And feet on the ground give me work to do!

There. That's one boot finished. I pick up the other, stopping a second to stretch my neck and to listen to the bob white practicing his song in the field behind the shop. The summer rhythm of his call always brings to my mind the sound of serves in a game of badminton: toss and swish, toss and swish. I gaze out the door at the green of June. Everything is growing splendidly after a rainy spring. God is creating a new heaven and a new earth, multiplying and making fruitful the seed He sowed. My fruitfulness is His work too. My work, even something as pragmatic as boot stitching, is not alien to the context. The Father's sustaining hand gives mine the ability to push the awl through the sole and thread the stitch through the loop. His love makes me to "be" minute by minute. For me, to stitch soles makes a simple whole with the growing of the grass and the shining of the sun. In union with Jesus, my Father works and I work, and the Kingdom comes an atom closer.

Boot number two is finished, and I put the pair in my basket with a little glow of satisfaction at a job done. I think of my sister, who will be glad to find her repaired boots under her locker, if not positively surprised to get them back after only two months' wait, and smile to myself. On to another pair that awaits my attention, with the uppers cracked and gaping in a couple of places.

This is a patching job. I cut and fit the patches, and glue them into place. While waiting for the glue to dry, I set up several more jobs: a sandal strap to be mended, a rubber boot to be sealed. And so the afternoon goes by.

The barn bell is old and cracked. It hangs from a post near the barn on a little green knoll where the road forks. It is rung by grasping the clapper and bumping it against the sides of the bell, making a dullish clanging. Not beautiful, but it tells us what we need to know: time to wind up the task in hand and get ready to go home. At least one summer, wasps were found nesting in the bell, rendering its ringing a heroic undertaking. Though the nest was sprayed, we never knew until we rang the bell whether or not an unhoused wasp had returned to check out the old homestead. The sister who is ringing today has no such qualms. She gives the bell a series of good whacks of the clapper, so that the garden sisters will hear, and someone cutting the grass in the orchard won't miss the signal.

I put away a few tools and load up my basket and step outside the door. People are heading back to the monastery from all the various employments. We walk back more or less together. The big bell from the monastery begins to ring for the end of work. Its sound reaches us wherever we are, calling us home, calling us to rest; the diastolic phase that is both end of one beat and beginning of another. Its note is beautifully firm and round with a resonance after each stroke. Inside, the bell ringer gives one last pull and stops the bell. The resonance of the last stroke goes from mezzo forte to pianissimo on its way to silence.

There's a basic rhythm in our life. It sings in my blood, in the in and out of my breathing. The bell has externalized it for a moment, as the bob white did earlier. Arsis and thesis: the stroke and arrest of stroke, sound and silence, work and rest. The measured alternation makes a whole, congruent in its small way with a higher wholeness, which is so whole it is at once perfect act and perfect rest.

This is a way of love, a way of knowledge, not just on the level of the intellectual, but also the somatic. We learn to love with our whole beings, to live out our love in every aspect of our lives, even the most material. We learn to listen for the quiet pulse of God's life in everything, and to enter into His rhythm. The rhythm in the depths of the Trinity is a heartbeat, the sound of the circulation of love. We become as cells dancing with unconcealed joy in the flow of Divine life, carrying secret health to members of the Mystical Body we may never know, but embrace unseen in faith and prayer.

III

HEAVEN OPENED

(August)

It's very hot and humid this afternoon. August is usually like that on our hill. The grass is parched and crunches under my feet as I turn off the road, even though there's plenty of moisture in the atmosphere. The sky overhead hangs like an over ripe fruit, thin-skinned and bulging. I hope that skin will split with lightning and lovely crashes of thunder tonight, setting free the needed rain . . . but not until the hay is in. Br. Dominic is out bailing now, and everyone who can go will stop her regular work and come to help bring in the hay as soon as he has it ready. It must be good, sweet, well-cured hay after this dry spell, with that delicious scent appreciated almost as much by human beings as by cows. It's going to be sweltering in the hay barn, though, where the stacks of hay grow slowly. Stacking is one activity that is almost worth the effort because of the relief of stopping. The atmosphere between loads is deeply peaceful. Everybody collapses on the nearest bale. The barn swallows swoop through the long streamers of light that flood down from two high windows. We watch a cat play with a piece of hay. Everybody is together, resting, in a very simple, elemental prayer of gift. It's not thought out, reasoned, measured—it's just gift—God's atmosphere of gift which we know.

The shoe shop has its own atmosphere. It welcomes me as I walk in the door, gives me the kiss of peace, and settles down to keep me company as I work—even on a torrid August day, even when I've had a hectic morning or have a problem on my mind. Somehow, it isn't long before my spirit lightens, and I find myself singing over the boots, joining in a song that was here before I came and will not cease when I leave. Here, Jesus lets me find Him in an oblique sort of way—an awareness of Him that is keener precisely in the degree that I am satisfied to let it be oblique. I enter into this afternoon, this smell of shoe shop, this ray of sun slanting over the lathe as I hold a sole to its sanding, this special presence of the Lord.

God's goodness to me perdures in this room, building on the prayer of the sisters who worked here before me. The first time I walked into it, it had the feel of a place that holds a Jacob's ladder. There are places like this all over our monastic enclosure, so many that they run into each other, creating an atmosphere vibrant with God. Angels tap on our awareness in the most unlikely spots, as we grow in sensitivity to their presence.

Moments of human honesty and the Lord's mercy, the overwhelming of poverty with God-gift, open from time, but which are outside of its tyranny. They are real prayer, and real prayer is contact with the God who Is. Moments must pass for us, but not for Him. We cannot maintain our attention unbroken, even to the radiant presence of God, but He has no such problem in our regard. The moment of prayer in which I am overwhelmed with my Father's gratuitous love is precious to Him, too, and perdures, marking the spot where it happened. That place becomes a Bethel, not only for the original "Jacob," but for others as well. I know that someone else's moment of truth before God burns here in the shoe shop, because its radiance shines across me as quietly as sunlight whenever I am still enough inside to be receptive.

A more familiar example of this enduring atmosphere of prayer is found in a church. It embraces those who love God, however obscure that love, and whether or not they understand what it is they sense in the place. It maddens those who hate God, so that they lash out in fury, being threatened in their fragile house of unbelief by something outside their rational control. The atmosphere of prayer clings to a ruined church or monastery, even centuries after the buildings have fallen into disuse.

In a monastery every place becomes church. People are always praying wherever they are, whatever they're doing, and

practically every day the Lord is breaking through for someone
in that special moment of truth. The scriptorium burns with His
Word, the woods are full of God. If I walk into the hermitage, I'm
met by a place that knows the Lord. It is awash with His love
and joy. It knows His mercy.

This phenomenon certainly is not limited to cloistered monks
and nuns. It is happening to people all over the world, in the
most varied environments. There is no specific difference. The
difference is in concentration and consequent intensity. The monastic atmosphere is so thick you can float in it. It holds you up.
It is so palpable it can strike visitors almost as a physical wave.
It can lift them up in a moment of clarity, giving them the perspective to recognize the presence of Jesus in their own lives and
in the world, to know the impossible as possible, the unbearable
as somehow again bearable.

A crash of thunder shatters my meditation, bringing me
abruptly to the thought of brother's hay. We're going to have to
run for it. Sure enough, there's a knock on the screen door, and
urgent signs that we're going to hay *now*. People are coming at
a run, and trailers are being hitched to tractors. The shoe shop
does not mind being thus precipitously abandoned. It will be
here tomorrow and the next day and until it is torn down, as
some day it must be. And even then, I wouldn't be surprised if
the angels remain in the area where it stood.

The bed of the GMC is packed with sisters. Someone reaches
a hand to late comers to clamber up and join us. We're off to the
hayfield as the first cool drops of rain prick our hot skin.

At the field we work quickly, in a pattern of bunching, load-
ing and stacking, and then we're headed back for the barn. As
the next to last trailer is being unloaded, the raindrops come more
quickly and the thunder is all around us. A few sisters scurry to
cover the last trailer with plastic sheets, and only just in time.

We get thoroughly soaked coming back from the barn. Some
run through the downpour, others walk along calmly, since
they're already wet through, enjoying the feel and smell of the
rain. If it keeps up during the interval before Vespers, I know
there will be a line of rain watchers along the open cloister. Some
will make a pretense of reading, but the books will soon lie for-

gotten on their laps, as they stare out into the downpour, fascinated by the sheer superabundance of this elemental gift. Each drop brings refreshment, beauty, and life. Billions of transparent tongues sing, whisper, shout in the grass, billions of little flames dance on the flagstones and make a splash-riot of the surface of the fish pool. The level of the fish pool rises, and the fish are gold flashes at the surface, exulting in the troubling of the roof of their world.

Worship, after all, can be as simple as grass drinking in the rain, as fish leaping in their proper element; as simple as the glad response of receiving in an atmosphere saturated with gift.

IV

INDEED YOU LOVE TRUTH

(October)

Sr. Marietta's shoe toes need patching. Perhaps she does chironomy with her big toe when she sings, but more likely she dances one toe's worth at times when the rest of her must be a bit more staid. It doesn't take much to make her dance with more than her toe, I reflect with a grin. I'll try to make the patch blend in well so it won't spoil the looks of her shoes. And Sr. Damian needs her run-over heels fixed again—the ones she wears to walk in the woods with our dog, Taffy. Taffy comes to life when she sees Sr. Damian or Sr. Henriette or Reverend Mother, in fact especially Mother. Sr. Henriette means food, brushing, and loyal defense of reputation; Sr. Damian means walks in the woods, tricks and treats; Mother means a special appreciation of her Taffyness that makes her tingle from end to wavering end. The rest of us aren't worth a wag most of the time.

The faces of my sisters come to my mind's eye. How different they are! To an outsider, I suppose one Trappistine looks much like the next, especially from a little distance. There couldn't be a greater illusion. "It takes all kinds to make a world," as the cliché goes. The monastery is a small world, and it is made up of as many kinds of people as there are sisters.

The way of Cistercian contemplative life seems to bring out each person's originality. The wonderful variety that results isn't explained by cultivated individualism—really the expression of underlying destitution—but by the living of an authentic spiritual life. Genuine originality is unselfconscious fidelity to truth. God has a unique idea in creating each of His children, and the more a person advances in the way of truth, the more the richness and unrepeatable specialness of that idea becomes manifest in her personality.

Sr. Luanne's organ shoes have the inner corner of the heels worn right off from pedaling. The shoes are ready to discard, but she begged me to fix them if possible, since they have the narrow heel and toe combination she needs for playing the organ. She likes thin soles, so as to be able to feel the pedals, so I won't replace these, even though they are nearly going into holes. I pry off the worn lifts reflectively, thinking of the beautiful music that pours out of sister through her nimble feet and hands.

Each pair of shoes I pick up has its own tale to tell. It might seem that the wearing of a habit, the following of a structured religious life, and especially the embracing of another's will in obedience would result in a lot of little robots. Not so. The result is rather a freedom to give our attention and energy to the things of the spirit, specifically to prayer. Prayer gradually clears our inner vision, makes us sensitive to what is false in ourselves, and—by the experience of the love and mercy of Jesus—gives us the courage to let go of the illusions we clutch to hide our failings.

What started me on this train of thought today? It was the shoes, surely, and the sisters they evoke for me. But it had already been simmering in my mind when I took the longer way over to the shoe shop, through the candy house shortcut, so that I could admire the line of trees where the edge of the woods meets the garden field. Autumn in New England puts on quite a show, and that particular vista is always a breathtaking sweep of color against the still emerald meadow. The sight jogged my memory of last hermit's day, when I sat out in the woods on a pile of lichened rocks and had time to think long thoughts. It had been one of those clear, fresh days that are the jewels of this month. The late afternoon sun had set the leaves on fire, and the trees were almost too bright to look at steadily. Each was different in shades of color, arrangement of branches and general shape. I studied a red-leafed maple. I noticed the way it came up out of the ground, and spread its limbs. I touched its bark, and thought about its history. I imagined it sprouting from a little winged seed, and growing around the pebbles in the soil where it had taken root. I thought of days and seasons and years that had gone by in its life—of the many variables that influenced its growth. But these accidentals only increased a difference that was there from the beginning. It was itself and no other.

But, I thought, the truth goes farther than that. There are no ditto marks in the whole landscape. Each leaf of every tree is a little different from every other leaf, even of the same tree. The mind has to stop. It can't deal with anything as uncountable as that.

Plunging into a concept too big for my limited intelligence to grasp is another way into prayer. Such thoughts run like powerful rivers into the awareness of God, the mystery of God. It's an easy way, too, because there is no dearth of dizzying facts ready to hand. Human relationships, stars at night, snow in winter are quite ordinary, at least on the surface; but the thought of the size of the universe, for example, or of the blizzard's worth of snowflake patterns in which there are no duplications, or of all the interweavings of Providence that brought this particular instant of my life to cross with this particular instant in yours and all the consequent ramifications: these things baffle my reason. My mind is swept totally out of its depth, and its incessant chatter submerged in the waters of wonder.

After I'd admired the trees in general from my vantage point, I had wandered through the woods, picking up leaves, and looking for unusually beautiful ones. My way lay along the brook that is a rushing torrent in the spring, shooting over the rocks below Mount Haig and foaming away in miniature rapids. At this season it is only a series of small puddles, hardly stirred by the slight movement of water seeping where gravity leads. I was dizzy with the beauty on all sides, and even more with the beauty of God. Even the still puddles reflecting the sky and mirroring the overhanging leaves were wells of vision to me. I walked slowly, following paths I know as well as the back of my hand, finding them fairytale-new. My leaf collection grew.

If you've ever looked for perfect fall leaves, you know there really aren't any. Each leaf seems to have some tiny defect on close inspection. Life has left its marks. I sat on one of the old, dry, stone walls that run through the woods to admire my leaf bouquet. The colors seemed duller, and the holes bugs had chewed blemished even the loveliest. But then I held a yellow leaf up to the sun, and it was immediately transformed. I found myself holding a haloed flame. The bug hole I had thought to disfigure the leaf sparkled as a diamond of pure light where the sun itself shone through unimpeded, and brilliant sun rays perfected its jagged edges. Once again my inner being stood still.

But not for long. My hermit thoughts began to meander along again, quietly, moving from leaves to people, especially the people I live with. It would be hard to miss the parable involved—as surely one of the Lord's as those in the Gospels. He teaches still. Because these wonderful people, these people I love, aren't perfect. Life has had its storms for each one and wounds of one kind or another have left scars. But when God's love shines through them, they are almost too beautiful to look at. The locus of the greatest injury or fault is just where the glory of His mercy shines most blindingly.

One of the keenest joys I've known in religious life, as I have experienced it in a community in which everyone is engaged in the search for God, is the thrill of seeing a person change under the influence of grace. We know each other very well because we live so closely together, and each person's principal faults are no secret. We pray for each other, we bear with each other, and then one day someone doesn't react in the old, expected way, or comes out with such a humble and insightful acknowledgment of her weaknesses that we are brought up short with her beauty. The realization that she is overcoming the fault that has always been her waterloo touches us to the quick, for we are part of each other's battles. To see this happening in another is to experience the hand of the Lord stretched out in His redeeming work. We aren't just contingent; we overlap, we are involved. Though only He can love redemptively, He lets us be channels of His love to each other—loving into realization the latent good in another, believing in the good that is not apparent as yet, but will be when the other has the courage to accept herself and Jesus' forgiveness. He widens our hearts to love unconditionally.

We also know that what appears in another is only the proverbial tip of the iceberg. Each human being is a private world.

Each is the partner in a special relationship with God, which has never been before and will never be duplicated. Respect and even a shy reverence is the natural concomitant to the contemplation of another person. Our eyes having been thus opened, it is no longer possible to take any human being for granted. There is no such thing as an ordinary person.

The Lord's compositions are very striking, I muse, filing the new lifts on Sr. Luanne's shoes. Who would think that orange and purple, scarlet and yellow would blend? In the autumn leaves they are daringly combined to create a symphony of color. The very clash of hues creates interesting harmony. None of us came to this community after studying each sister in it and choosing everyone as being just to her liking and the perfect answer to all her needs. But God did that in His own way. He chose each of us for this monastery, and this monastery for each of us; each sister for me and vice versa. Precisely the one I might not have chosen, God may have chosen to be the catalyst of a breakthrough on which the very fruition of my contemplative life depends.

The Holy Spirit's work in a soul is very delicate and secret. He knows exactly what is really needed, and brings about in His own time the changes that will constitute the perfection of each of us, given only our good will. He has His ways of keeping our attention away from the essential work He is doing in our depths, often by spotlighting some habitual flaw. If we were not humbled and kept busy by the battle with such faults, we would spoil everything by jumping in and trying to help God with our myopic ideas of perfection, ruining the fine adjustments only He can make.

Once I had a dream about the community, a dream that stuck in my memory. We were out in the open cloister—a walkway that forms one side of our monastery quadrangle—and we were walking at random and singing. We weren't paying any attention to one another, but just wandering, looking at the flowers in the garth and the sky. We were singing a beautiful piece of music in many parts—as many as there were sisters. I was aware that we were learning the music, singing it for the first time, but not from notations on paper. We were clearly being taught, each one from within herself, and yet it was all coming out in exquisite harmonies. The music was not ours. It was being given to us note by note. My part was difficult. I had to put forth my best effort to sing the high notes. I woke up with the words still running through my head, and recognized them as part of Psalm 94 with which we begin Vigils every day: "For He is our God, and we, the people He pastures, the flock that is led by His hand." The dream didn't fade as quickly as dreams usually do because it symbolized our Cistercian life so powerfully. We were together, yet alone; supporting and blending with each other, yet each one singing her own part.

A corollary is that if we don't sing our own part, it just isn't there. It isn't replaced because it can't be. A certain tiny richness that should have been is gone from the music of humanity. God's composition isn't ruined, but to His infinite ear, a sound He planned isn't there, and it matters.

I have to sing the music I am being taught, not that given to someone else, no matter how much I admire the latter. But I am part of all others' music, and they are part of mine, for we make a polyphonic whole. Sr. Luanne's skilled fingers and feet are mine, and Sr. Marietta's dancing. If Taffy runs to greet Sr. Damian with bright eyes and wagging tail, I share. After all, I have mended my sisters' shoes, if nothing else, and I have loved them.

V

ALL IN ALL

(November)

One of the things our contemplative life gears us to recognize is that nearly everything in our common, human experience is sacramental. Experiences, people, things, have their own meaning, but beyond that there is a deeper meaning, which is not less but more real. The deeper meanings of everything converge. As we become sensitized to the sacred level, life and prayer become increasingly simple. The path of all events is followed inward, and the eyes of the heart gaze toward the point where all things meet. God Himself, we see, holds the ultimate meaning of everything in His love.

It is a daily adventure, this search for sacramentals. It's a bit like those puzzles that contain hidden pictures or messages. I look and look and look, and suddenly the picture jumps out at me from what was previously a meaningless muddle. And the most exciting aspect about it is that one deeper meaning isn't the end of it. Hours, days, or perhaps years later, the first deeper reality of something will suddenly split open to reveal something yet more profound. Words become inadequate, and I stand in full and singing silence, knowing truth which concepts cannot capture.

A few years ago I received a letter, written in November, in which my correspondent described this month in New England as "bleak." It shocked me. November is anything but bleak to me. I love each season as it comes along, for each has its own outer beauties and inner messages. It is true that November colors are subdued—brown, gray, olive drab. Only the evergreens have living color left. But this tending toward monotone is convergence. The fields and woods have moved from last month's flamboyant diversity toward unity, or rather, the underlying unity that always existed is revealed now that October's gorgeous fires have died down. This is the end of the season, or . . . its highest development. The simple precedes the complex, and reappears as final resolution. Unity is more basic than complexity.

Lack of colors also heightens artfulness of line. Bare trees have their own austere beauty, and so does the bony land. If I stand on a knoll in the woods I can see the shape of the land running down to the brook and up the opposite incline as I cannot when the trees are in leaf. And I can see through the filigree of branch tips to the distant blue bowl of hills that rim our horizon on south and east. We ourselves are on the northwest rim of the same blue bowl. It all connects. It all connects, and everything that connects is sacramental of that unity in God which is creation's inmost truth.

It's not only the natural world that intimates our unity at this season. The theme of the liturgy also gathers toward fullness. November is the month of all the saints. Besides the Church's feast of All Saints on November 1, we of Saint Benedict's great family have our feast of All the Saints of the Order on November 13. They encircle us. We are one with them, though they have gone out of sight toward the glowing heart of Reality. It is no coincidence that the Church's year will close at the end of this month with the feast of Christ the King, because it is in Him that everything comes together. He is the great bond of connection, the crown of all the saints, the summing up of all creation.

It is also a good time for cleaning the shoe shop, and taking stock. Suppose the Lord should ask me to render an account of my cobblership tonight. I wouldn't like to have to admit that I can't remember when I last oiled the lathe, but that it was so long a time ago; or that I've let my cousins, the spiders (ah yes, we are related, however distantly), build their webs in all the corners. I wouldn't want Him to notice the wasps' nest suspended from the frame of my back window, or the little pieces of dirty cork from the sole filler of someone's footwear littering the floor around the shoe last.

My duster is a piece of green and black checked wool. I ply it vigorously, and a spider family scurries for the cracks, as their web home becomes a dirty gray ball. Never mind, spiders! I'm sure you're on to me sufficiently to know you can rebuild in a few days, out of that marvelous architectural genius God made instinctual in you. And then you can live securely to see your children's children before I go on another cleaning spree.

My duster moves busily on, and my thoughts turn to Fr. Anselm. The connection is obvious to anyone who knew him during the later years of his chaplaincy here. The cloth is a piece of his old blanket—not a blanket from his bed, but a blanket he *wore*—on top of his hooded jacket and several other layers of clothing—to keep warm. His circulation was poor, and he was always cold. That didn't keep him from sitting in the often drafty outer chapel, though, for every Hour of the Divine Office. Fr. Anselm wasn't shy about that blanket, either. He'd stand up, wrap it around himself with a flourish, pin it with a large safety pin, and sit down with the gracious air of the perfectly poised. Or it would be better to say, the gracious air of the perfectly simple in the spiritual sense of that definition, for Fr. Anselm had reached that stage of spiritual convergence. He died with felicitous timing on November 13, feast of all the Blessed who "fought under the Rule of Saint Benedict."

The wasps in the papery nest in the window have become whatever wasps become in winter, so it's safe to flick away the little cluster of tubes. I bet Fr. Anselm could make a sparkling sermon even on the theme of wasps' nests. He had various techniques for his talks—all lively and fashioned to fix the point in the memories of his hearers. There were sermons on Snoopy, and sermons on his birthday psalm; sermons on some bit of poetry picked up in *Christopher News Notes*, and slogan words, each letter of which stood for a virtue to be practiced. His speech was picturesque. None of us will forget the "houses to let on Thankfulness Avenue for anyone who'd like to move off Grumbly Street," or "chin up, cheerio, and carry on." And surely Cherry Belle radishes and marigolds—"Mary's gold"—will ever evoke Fr. Anselm for me. A favorite of mine among his methods, though, was the building of a talk on dictionary definitions.

As a matter of fact, that's another reason for Fr. Anselm to be on my mind this afternoon. Just last week I tried that method, not for a sermon, of course, but just for my own benefit, looking up word definitions on a theme in the best approved Anselmian way. And to be sure, unity was the theme of the words I chose, sleuthing my intuition that they all met richly in God: exciting words like "individual" and "integrity," "authenticity" and "originality."

Well, Fr. Anselm, since you seem to be with me this afternoon, I might as well share with you the fruit of my dictionarial explorations, while continuing this most necessary cleanup. You'd expect words of the family I mentioned to lead in the direction of diversity, wouldn't you? But among the definitions given for each word, I found enough basis for a strong case in the opposite direction. Take the word "originality" for example. We ordinarily think of originality as being that which is different, unique. But "originality" comes from "original," which bears the meaning "of, *relating to*, or constituting an origin or beginning." "Origin" is "the point at which something begins its course or existence." So . . . to be really original is to relate to God our Origin. All our originalities meet in Him. Isn't that beautiful? "Authenticity" is another gorgeous word. I found this among its definitions: "fidelity to actuality and fact—conforming to an original so as to reproduce essential features." The actuality, the fact, is that God is our Author. Authenticity is to say with our whole lives the message He wants us to incarnate, the inmost secret of our personalities. And that message is basically the same for all—love—because that's God's essential feature. "God so loved the world . . . ,"and we are to be like our Heavenly Father. It follows that our relationship to the world must be just like His. Love unites—to God, and to all God's creation.

We think of an "individual" as standing apart from others, but really the word means undividable, "an indivisible entity." This has much more to do with wholeness, singleness or purity of heart than might be apparent from the common use of the term. It's almost like a koan.

The more original and authentic I am, the more faithfully do I express my Father's intention, and the more truly individual

I am, the closer I am to all humanity: e.g. (and this is really *exempli gratia!*), after Jesus, our Lady was the most original of human beings precisely because everything in her was total *yes* to God. By the intense union of her most pure heart with the Author of us all, by making Him her all, she is present to all generations not as remote model but as living Mother.

"Integrity" is another one I looked up. It is from the Latin *integer*, which means "whole, entire." The dictionary included under its definition, "the quality or state of being undivided . . . unity." To be a person of integrity is to be all of one piece, with no façade. It is to be before others what one is before God. "Genuine" is "accordance with an original, sincerity," and "veritable" is "correspondence with truth, suggestion of affirmation." Jesus is the Truth in the most radical sense, and affirmation means *yes*.

How's that, Fr. Anselm? I bet you inspired it! Many people have enriched my life, and you are certainly among them. No reason to suppose you've stopped, now that your life is deeper, richer, stronger than it could be while hindered by mortality. The unity of the communion of saints assures me that your wholeness can help me toward wholeness, toward being more wholly God's.

Being wholly God's is expressed in monastic language as "purity of heart." There may be areas of purity right from the beginning—indeed there must be, for the call to be heard and answered—but true Christ-centeredness of life doesn't come easily. All the diverse elements of one's personality realign, under the influence of prayer and through the work of grace, only little by little. But the time comes when there cease to be dichotomies even in the matter of work and prayer, silence and necessary speech, Divine Office and simple contemplation, because the primary dichotomy in the personality has been dissolved in Christ. In the end, one's will is totally absorbed in His *yes* to the Father.

Paradoxically enough, it is on this personal level that a contemplative experiences most vitally her unity with all mankind. Perhaps that's why the most vivid awareness of solidarity may occur in solitude—in the hermitage perhaps, or in the woods, or . . . in the shoe shop. I am not alone here. I am the Church; I am the human race with all its weaknesses and sins, with all its highest aspirations. The villain of the piece is here: that self that seeks its own in everything. But the real hero, Jesus, is even closer. His love working in me is intended to break down my walls. His love in me wants to reach out to others, to give back to the Father unreservedly, in the simultaneous two-way current that is the Spirit. I must be clean of heart, well-oiled of will, so that God can move me as He wills.

The thought of cleaning and oiling returns me abruptly to the material plane, and the waiting lathe. I need to put a new piece of emery cloth on the heel grinder, too. The old piece is so worn it's on the point of breaking. Better to change it before it snaps while the lathe is running. A broken piece slapping the wheel cover makes an enormous roar. The last time it happened, Br. Dominic came running to ask, "What happened?" and "Are you all right?"

My mind moves appreciatively from Br. Dominic and Fr. Anselm to Br. Matthew and Fr. David, and all the monks who share with us the tremendous grace of Cistercian monastic vocation. The personalities of the four I happen to know best are very different, even though Fr. Anselm was Br. Matthew's blood brother; and yet there is such unity in their ideal, such love of the life to which God called them. The differences are lovable; the unity palpable and supportive.

As a matter of fact, unity is a precious heritage of our Order. Our twelfth-century founders recognized it as a spiritual value we are called to express in a particular way, for the building up of the Church. This unity is a reminder of the apostolic community, and also a prophetic foreshadowing of the eschatological Church, when all will be subjected to Christ, and He will then "be subject in his turn to the One who subjected all things to him, so that God may be all in all."* This lived sacrament of unity is all the more complete and rich because we have the advantage of complementarity in our Order with its two branches. The blend of many cultures in an international Order

* 1 Corinthians 15:28, JB.

sets the theme of unity in bold relief. It is a wonderful experience to meet Cistercians from Japan, Germany, Spain, France, the Philippines, etc., with that instant recognition in others of one's own familial traits. It's not the habit or the customs, but the vision, the call, the spirituality that we recognize in one another.

In addition to this global unity, we have strong bonds between individual monasteries, especially founding houses and their daughter houses. But the strongest bond, and the most ordinary expression of unity, is that we daily find within the local community. It's not just a matter of smooth operation, or even of mutual spiritual and material support. It's not just a peaceful setting for individual contemplation. Unity is of the essence. It is one of those sacraments of deeper realities I was thinking about earlier this afternoon.

The abbess is the visible sign and foremost factor in the oneness of heart of her sisters. It is striking that, according to the Rule of Saint Benedict, she is "said to hold the place of Christ in the monastery." She brings the community together in her own heart, her own prayer, locking the whole into the Heart of Christ. Through her, the gifts and needs of each one are integrated into a whole, in which all are for each, and each for all.

I remember when the mystery of unity first broke open for me. It was during a community retreat. The retreat master was a monk from one of our Cistercian monasteries, and he spoke about unity in Cistercian life as a dynamic force, not as a static reality. It grows deeper and closer, and its depths open out into the mystery of the Trinity. It is a living out on the human plane of that most central mystery of our faith, a sacramental by which the Divine life is actually transposed into human terms. That life is love.

And His love is mighty. It is the great centripetal force that is drawing all time, all peoples, to itself, so that in the end God will be "everything to everyone."

This is how our unity here in the monastery serves the vital progress of the Church. We are a microcosm of the world, individually and as a community, and what happens here—even in this shoe shop, this hour—helps in some tiny degree to hasten the day when all will be one in that bliss that is our true end.

The setting sun sends a final orange ray over the straightened room. The dust I've stirred up dances in it. It is a fitting conclusion to the afternoon. At the end of his life, Saint Benedict has a vision of all creation in a single ray of light, a ray that symbolized Christ. As his followers, we live this mystery intensely, and find in it more joy than we can ever hold, more than enough for the entire world, which is God's point. God would share the perfect fullness of His joy with all, and it will be full for all when He is all in all.

VI

RADIANT WITH JOY

(December)

Sometime since yesterday afternoon, a roguish puff of wind tried my stovepipe for a trombone, and managed to blow out the pilot light. The shop is stone cold, calling for the stove-lighting ritual. I kneel beside the stove, light a match, reach around back of the stove with my left hand to depress and hold in the pilot knob, reach around the lower front of the stove with my right hand and apply the match. Blow out match. Say three Hail Marys slowly. With dial still held down I turn it, then release. Listen for hiss of gas and answering swish of flame. Hear the usual pop of pilot going out instead. Sometimes it takes five or six matches before the thermocouple is warm enough to stay open.

Hail Mary, full of grace. . . . Full of grace from your first moment, never a moment when you were not entirely open to God in every corner of your being. Full of waiting for whatever God might ask of you, full of patience, full of love. Dare I let go of the dial again? Another pop, another match. I lay my cheek against the stove in my awkward position of embrace. Mary, clean as snow, pure of heart, free, wide place, large enough for all the world. How glad I am that snow is falling outside! If it sticks there is a good chance we'll have a beautiful white world for December 8, for Mary . . . and for the profession. Happily, it looks sufficiently determined to provide at least a thin wedding garment. Mount Saint Mary's hilltop is turning Mary-white, Mary-white with diamonds. I know the diamonds are there, though I can't see them in the gray afternoon. They will wink out blue, red, green, gold reflected fire when the sun comes out.

"Behold the Bridegroom comes! Let us go out to meet Him!"* Now . . . a careful twist of the dial holding my mouth just so, and release. Ah, at last, the hiss, swish of ignition. I turn up the dial and unbend my stiff, cold knees.

Our Lady was always ready to catch fire the moment the flame was offered. She "held in her womb the burning coal," as our Advent canticle says, referring to the call of Isaiah: the fire to be cast on the earth, the conflagration that will make us pure again, the blaze that will never go out. This is Advent time— Isaiah time. We wait in joyful hope, living again that first Advent with Joseph and Mary and her hidden flame. The warmth poured out of her in radiant charity, in the sparkle of her eyes, in the lilt of her voice. Within his mother, John danced. Who would not dance at the sound of it? I dance just a little, once around the work table, ostensibly to get my feet warm, but really for Advent joy. "My soul magnifies the Lord, my spirit rejoices in God, my Savior!"**

My little stove is throwing out good heat now. Little stove, my prayer-fire is more similar to yours than like our Lady's: slow to light up and easily blown out by a small-sized storm. How often God is met with nothing but a pop of flame going out the second He withdraws the consolation that has set me burning. The wonder is that He keeps relighting me, and when lit, even a dented, old, gray stove can warm a small room.

I can discard my coat now, and get down to work. Yesterday I made the buckle for a new belt, and today I must cut the strap and put it together. I should have done it last week, but December is a busy time, and here it is the sixth already. The completed belt is to be blessed tomorrow, along with the new black scapular the wardrobe made. I try to clear sufficient space on the table, give it up as hopeless, and unroll the leather on the floor. A piece of wood goes under the leather. I measure out the belt carefully, making little pricks with the knife, and then set the metal T-square in place. It's hard to cut a belt really straight. It's hard at

---

* Antiphon for Song of Mary, 2nd Vespers, Common of Virgins.
** Luke 1:46-47, RSV.

any time, but the floor breathes cold and stiffens my fingers, despite the best efforts of the stove, rendering the job even more of a challenge. I press down on the T-square and draw my knife along its edge. The leather has a tendency to squirm away no matter how firmly I hold it. I might be able to cut straight if it was a matter of a single stroke, but it is not. The first stroke slices only the surface. It takes three or four strong cuts to get through the hide, and I can do only about nine inches at a time because that's all I can control firmly. Another nine inches follow, hoping it is in line with the previous, and so on.

This afternoon it strikes me as singularly appropriate for the commitment the belt will symbolize. My belts always have a few little "thank you ma'ams" where I didn't quite make the second stroke exact, or accurate connections, or (might as well be honest) where I substituted force for patience. Vows aren't a matter of one glorious day, followed by a straight course to heaven. It's a matter of many, many strokes, day after day, year after year. And because we are human, they aren't always in a straight line. The material we have to work with—ourselves—also shares in that squirming-away-from-the-knife property of belt leather. But as long as we don't give up, it will come out all right in the end—not because we are faithful, but because God is. Isaiah picturesquely says, "Faithfulness is the belt about His hips."* If our hearts are right, then the ups and downs (and downright flops) don't really change anything except (hopefully) our pride. It becomes obvious that we can promise steadfast love only because we are loved steadfastly.

There are two ways to live: wholeheartedly or less than wholeheartedly. In the cloister the choice means happiness or misery, a supremely worthwhile life or a waste of time, because radical gift is of the essence of the vocation. It isn't a case of black and white, though, but of lighter and lighter shades of gray. The choice must be repeatedly renewed, starting all over again every day, because our natural tendency is to take back a little here, and reserve a bit for ourselves there. To love steadfastly for us

---

* Isa 11:5, JB.

means to keep trying, to keep shoving off for the depths of self-forgetfulness, instead of living on the surface of life where the ego operates for its own advantage. Monastic life is set up to help us in this continual reorientation, and it is the subject of a special vow—that of *conversatio* which means fidelity to the monastic life, implying continual conversion. Like the other vows it helps us to grow.

Our sister preparing for vows is a rather skinny novice, so I have less to cut this time, though I leave a good tail for her to grow into. This job is a joy no matter what the girth of the sister destined to receive the belt as a sign of the vows she will have just made. The first vowed commitment to God in the monastic life of our community is a temporary one, but the heart knows no such juridical stipulations. By the time she comes to this step, the sister has been in monastic life long enough to have experience of her own weakness. The fact that she has hung on, in spite of the painful self-knowledge that begins in the novitiate through the deepening of prayer, is sure evidence that she has also known the power of Jesus working in her life, assuring her that He will complete what He has begun.

Surely He did begin it. Perhaps some people always wanted to enter religious life and followed eagerly the moment they perceived the first faint intimations of a call to the monastic life; but some kind of struggle is more common. The call cuts right across our plans and turns values upside down. But it is too deep, too dear, too true to our inmost dream to hold out against, and so we capitulate, and the first great rush of unexpected freedom sweeps us up in a tide of joy.

As with any human love, the first stages are more emotional, and postulants and novices usually go up and down at a dizzying rate. The novitiate knows much laughter . . . and many tears. Ecstatic heights and abysmal depths little by little level off as the spiritual gains ascendancy over the emotional. Real love grows; the kind of love that is absorbed in the Other to the point of at least occasional self-forgetfulness, a love that seeks to give without condition or reserve. This is inchoative purity of heart.

There, the strap is free now, and reasonably straight. The next step is to round off the tail, and skive the buckle end. Skiving is the beveling of an edge of leather, by cutting it at an angle from the underside so that the end is paper-thin and will make a smooth joint when glued to another piece. Since my mind is on the vows this afternoon, for obvious reasons, everything seems to have its point to make on the subject. We, too, have our corners to round off and our edges to bevel. Bumps dig into people uncomfortably, especially at close quarters! Conversion of manners can get very specific.

All this talk of belts and binding and cutting sounds so painful and restricting. And yet, paradoxically, living under vows has been for me a journey into freedom. I remember going right up to my profession thinking I was making a big sacrifice for love of God, binding myself hand and foot to be laid on the altar like Isaac. But during that retreat—I remember the exact spot because the impact was unforgettable—I was overtaken by such a rush of freedom that my whole life was lifted into another dimension. This experience of freedom was so different, so unbounded, that all previous content of the word for me appeared now only a travesty.

If only one could live on the crest! ("Lord, it is good for us to be here! Let us build three tabernacles. . . .""). But if we did we would never grow in love. Even our Lady, or should I say especially our Lady, had to go through troughs where nothing could be seen but a dark wall of water on either side, threatening to swamp her. Love is proved by a yes when one can't see.

I cut out a notch for the tongue of the buckle and thread the strap into place. Next is the glue to affix the skived end firmly in place. I add a large staple salvaged from a carton to reinforce the glue, and hammer down the metal ends tightly. Good. No strain on the buckle, no Christmas week expansion will make it give way. Vows put physical limits to our "horizontal" expansion. They are deliberately chosen means to growth in purity of heart, channels by which all our thrust is directed toward one end. Poverty sets our hearts free from a multiplicity of things, chastity from the many divisive pulls of the flesh, and obedience from

* Mark 9:5, free translation.

that most insatiable of slave drivers, self-will. The other specifically Benedictine vow, stability—which fixes us in a given geo-
graphical place, community, and way of life—frees us from the
"the grass is greener on the other side of the fence" syndrome,
and thus saves a lot of energy that would be dissipated fruitlessly
were we free to follow our demon desires for change. This vow
allows us to sink deep into prayer, especially the prayer that is
lived out in a whole lifestyle and a given situation. There is no
way to escape over or around difficulties; they must be faced and
gone through, if we are not to come to a complete halt. This is
precisely the process that grinds off the ego bumps we have on
ourselves so that our intent can become more and more purely
just to be for God and to love Him with our whole hearts.

Just the belt loop to do now, and that's an easy job — just
watch that I don't make it too tight for the tail to go through or too
loose to hold the end in place. The loop should have a relaxed grip.

The wind has ceased howling. I wonder if the snow has
stopped. It has stuck all over the screen of my back window and
effectively blocked the view. I can't resist opening the door to
take a look. The snow is falling heavily, but quietly now. It is
beautiful, beautiful. The soft lines of the white snow on the forsythia bushes remind me of the community putting on cowls for
choir. No cowl yet for my sister, but that will come with solemn
vows in a few years . . . for richer for poorer, in sickness and in
health. . . .

Back to my job after flexing my fingers for a moment at the
stove. Three holes to be punched with newly warmed fingers—
one hole for now, one for feasts, and one for leaner days. The
final touch; polish carefully rubbed in and buffed to a shine.
Mary, Mother of us all, model of monks (and monkesses!), be
with my little sister, especially as she begins her professed Cistercian life, and give your Mother's blessing to this belt I've made
for her. May it always remind her that if she is bound, it is with
love, and she is only girt to run the more freely in the ways of
the Lord. Saint Benedict says that as we advance, what was for-
merly difficult becomes sweet and easy, because of the greatness
of love, and he speaks truly. We wait in joyful hope, with the
waiting that is running.

Mount Saint Mary's people are turning Mary-white, Mary-white with diamonds. I can't see the diamonds in the early winter dusk, but I know they're there. And when the Son rises on the clean world, they will sparkle back His glory like uncountable Christmas lights. They are so eager, these young ones, so bright-eyed. But we, whose hair the years have sneakily begun to frost, we are not less eager; and the old are brightest-eyed of all.

VII

MANNA

(February)

The barn bell warning the approach of end of work surprises me. I'll have to look for a pair of substitute boots for Sr. Mary. Hers are in great need of repair again, and I haven't time to tackle them today. She works so hard that the soles melt down to nothing, the heels run over all the way to the soles on one side of each boot, and the uppers develop vast splits. The spare boots are stored in cartons under my work table. I poke hopefully into the top of the box marked 7, without pulling it out. No luck. There's nothing for it but to pull the heavy carton out so that I can open it properly, and start taking everything out of it. What I want will probably be found (with the perversity of inanimate objects) on the very bottom layer. I make a profound bow over the box. At this point a sigh would be appropriate. Instead, I find myself singing, gently, under my breath, as I do so often when I am alone at work. The melody just bubbles out, without premonition. "Man does not live on bread alone, but on every word that comes from the mouth of God."*

I don't have to go far to find the reason that particular antiphon should be in my mind today. This morning we practiced it at the regular Saturday singing practice for tomorrow, which is the First Sunday of Lent. It is wonderful to live on the Word of God—to take it in deeply, assimilate it, and have it rise up spontaneously from my own depths to embody thoughts and

* Matthew 4:4, JB.

reactions. And each time it comes up to conscious mind, it nour-
ishes, and whets my appetite for more.

The elusive boots are found at last, and loaded into the
basket for the trip home. I turn down the heat to night setting,
put on my coat, cap and mittens, and pick up the basket. In a
few minutes I'm stamping snow off my boots in the barn clothes
shed, and putting away my coat. The monastery still smells of
fresh bread from this morning's baking. I sniff gratefully as the
fragrance greets me. Saturday is baking day—raisin bread for
Sunday! The homely incense pervades the whole monastery—
wafting upstairs, stealing downstairs, and finding its way under
doors and around all obstacles, even into the basement shower
room.

The barn sisters have beaten me home, and the shower room
is already full of clouds of steam and the sound of running water.
"Not by bread alone . . ." There it is again, singing voicelessly
inside me, with that automatic adjustment to the presence of
others that we acquire in community life. The rushing noise of
showers merely gives it accompaniment. Floods of water do not
drown it, I reflect, enjoying my own ablutions. The unpremedi-
tated swipe from the Song of Songs in such incongruous applica-
tion tickles my sense of humor. But such swiping is in a great
tradition. I'm sure that's the way the Cistercian Fathers wrote.
Scripture quotes came out of them spontaneously, adapted to
contexts quite different from their original matrix. Surely the
Fathers didn't write with the thought that quoting Scripture is
pious, and therefore they must quote Scripture, must dig out
biblical language and force their thought into it. No, quite simply,
their minds were full of the Word of God.

Saint Benedict, following the Fathers of the desert, pre-
scribed a most efficacious means for reaching such fullness: the
Divine Office spaced throughout the day. As his followers we,
like the Cistercian Fathers before us, find that the language of
Scripture kneaded into our minds at regular intervals becomes
second nature, offering itself as vessel for our thoughts. Day after
day at Vigils, Lauds, Terce, Mass, Sext, None, Vespers and Compline we are filled with good things, and our memories store this
food of the spirit to be carried with us at all times.

I remember the glow I felt when this prescription first began to work for me. It wasn't very long after I entered monastic life, but long enough for the Word to have entered my bloodstream through *lectio* and participation in the Work of God, as Saint Benedict termed the Liturgy of the Hours. One morning after Vigils when I looked out the cloister windows at the stars pulsing in their constellations, familiar since early childhood, instead of "twinkle, twinkle little star" or some other inanity, there came to my inner ear, "When I consider the heavens, the work of Your fingers, the moon and the stars which You have made, what is man that You are mindful of him? Or the son of man, that You visit him?"* The wonder of the psalmist at God's concern with insignificant me, at His mercy, became my own wonder. I was thrilled. And then it happened at work too.

The Word of God is alive. It acts in us like yeast. The living, unpredictable aspect of God's Word is what fuels the anticipation I feel at the approach of a new liturgical season. No matter how many times I've sung the proper Lenten antiphons and listened to the assigned Lenten readings, they are never the same. I have no idea what kind of bread the Lord will make for me out of the familiar words.

My shower over, I head for the Scriptorium. I have to do my little part, which is to look up the ingredients for tomorrow's liturgy. The recipe for the First Sunday of Lent is from Genesis, 1 Peter and Mark. I will read the assigned texts slowly, letting them sift through my mind, but not trying to search out meanings. This is not the time for exegesis. I have a rich accumulation of associations which the Lenten liturgy recalls, but I don't try to refresh myself on past insights. I let them act and react as they will, under the impulse of the Holy Spirit. New meanings will erupt, new manna will fall.

There's the first bell for Vespers already. As I go into chapel, I think of the old Latin long responsory we no longer use. *Paradisi portæ* ("the gates of paradise") is hardly what one would expect at the outset of this penitential season, but it is the true

---

* Psalm 8; *The Grail Psalter*.

keynote to strike. What Lent means is return to the Father whom we love. That is why Saint Benedict would have the life of his monks be a continual Lent. The way lies through the desert— true— but He is always sending His angels to care for us, and spreading manna for our food while we sleep. And sooner or later we come to the mountain of God, and He makes Himself known to us in a gentle breeze, and we have no need of other food until we find ourselves on the plain again. The Promised Land, it is said, flows with milk and honey. But we have our desert Horebs, our foretastes.

The big bell peels in formal announcement of Vespers. We stand to begin with the sign of the cross and the verse, "O God, come to my assistance. . . ." As we bow profoundly for the *Gloria,* the angels, too, are bowing. The Rule reminds us that we are always in their presence, but especially when we are praising God in choir. Some ancient paintings show an angelic choir above a monastic choir, and stories about angels—replacing martyred monks or being seen among nuns singing the Office—abound. These are medieval legends, no doubt, but they embroider a profound truth. Monastic life exists to adore God. This is not just primary; it's our whole purpose. We are consecrated to this. Monastic life is called "the angelic life" not because monks (either sex) are angels, or even especially good men and women, but because we are consecrated to the perpetual praise of God. This is a praise that is not just dutiful, but an invaluable privilege.

The angels are like laser beams—love concentrated into the now that is their forever. But we are embodied creatures, subject to time. Among us, the martyrs at the moment of their death come closest to the angels in totality of worship. We may not choose martyrdom as a deliberate goal, but there is another way. We can spread adoration over every minute and every action of our lives by intention, since our frailty does not permit incessant consciousness, and we can try to ratify it by the way we live.

By the same token, we can do what the angels cannot. We have our weakness to offer. Our very frailty occasions the return to God that glorifies His mercy. The plaintive melody of the Lenten Vespers hymn sets in minor key the theme that will burst forth in its final major on Holy Saturday evening: "O happy fault, that merited such a redeemer!'"* And the angels do not share a corporeal body and subjection to time, as we do, with all visible creation, animate and inanimate. Therefore they must entrust to us the worship of God that gathers the universe to bow before the Trinity. Our love incorporates the unconscious yearnings of beasts and flowers, mountains and seas, from yeast cell to farthest star.

Another bow for the doxology of the hymn sweeps over the choir. This bow, as that for the *Gloria,* is kin to my earlier bow over the barn boot box. My life is of a piece, and any act good or indifferent in itself becomes a gesture of adoration. Monastic life is indeed an anticipation of heaven. It's a rather busy heaven to be sure. Bread to make, cows to milk, shoes to mend—even the liturgy takes a lot of work.

The liturgy room is a small beehive. There's always someone in there typing, filing readings, or running off music or canticles on the copier. Usually there are several bodies in the tiny room, amicably digging their elbows into each other in their efforts to accomplish various jobs in close quarters. Our liturgy commission has about a dozen enthusiastic members. When they have one of their creative meetings in the chapter room to plan some ceremony or troubleshoot the Liturgy in general, they sound like fifty people having an exciting time. They emerge all aglow, and one speeds off to the computer. We are not kept long in suspense, as the notices are soon papering the wall in the spot where such things are posted. Everything is chosen with great care to fit feast or season. But within this human work, this human choice, is the choice of the Lord. It is He who stands and feeds His sheep— sometimes through others, sometimes directly.

Psalm 144 was not especially chosen for today, let alone for me in particular. It is a regular part of Saturday Vespers, Week 2. How is it, then, that as the verses come along, some jump out at me to underline my thoughts? "The eyes of all creatures look to you, and you give them their food in due time. You open wide your hand, grant the desires of all who live."** He who knows me

---

* *Exsultet*, Liturgy for Holy Saturday of the Great Week.
** Psalm 144:15-16; *The Grail Psalter.*

from the inside, who knows every experience of my life, every desire of my heart, selected this psalm for this moment. It is as personal as that. Jesus opens the Scriptures in the mystery of His living presence.

The desert looms ahead. Its primary message is dependence on God for whatever is necessary. The desert is full of eyes, looking to Him. He stretches wide His hands (and now I see Jesus on the cross) and grants the real desire of all who live. The Spirit flows from His Heart.

The psalmody ends with a doxology. Everything we do begins and ends so, bowing low within the great adoration of the Word made Flesh—Jesus. We live under the same roof with Him in the Blessed Sacrament, which is the Mass in concentrated form—that is, it is Jesus in His total offering to the Father on Calvary, His perfect act of love. In this He reveals the Father to us.

The Divine Office is not just a setting for the Mass. It is the extension of the Mass over every corner of the day, every event and human emotion. Vigils, Lauds and Terce look forward to it; Sext, None, Vespers and Compline savor it, look back on it, to "thank and thank and thank," in Fr. Anselm's characteristic phrase. In all these and in the first part of the Mass the Lord feeds us with His Word. And then He gives us His Body and Blood in direct transfusion of Life. We are truly fed. The bread of angels has become the bread of man, even of the poor, weak sinners that we are, utterly incapable of perfect love or undistracted worship.

A reading, a silent pause, a recited canticle, leads up to the climactic moment for the *Magnificat*. With our Lady we praise the Father who has filled the starving with good things. The beauty of the music lifts me in its simple power—beauty like salt that adds savor to the food of the spirit. The music itself is prayer. Quite aside from the words that are carried on the peaceful waves of plainchant, the prayerfulness of this ancient music is tangible. But it was meant to be a setting for words, it is ordained to a text, giving interpretation, revealing depths and connections that would escape notice in a mere reading.

To praise God is to be fed, to be fed is to magnify the mercy of the Lord. Our praise adds nothing to Him, but it opens us to receive His grace, His love, His life, and that is His glory. He would have it spread to a great multitude.

Now only one voice is heard. Our abbess says the Our Father. At other times we all say the Our Father together, but at Lauds and Vespers Saint Benedict would have us listen—for a very specific reason. Our community life is close—inevitably in a situation where you're rubbing elbows, there's going to be occasional friction. Our human faults are all too apparent. We can't avoid tripping over other people's mistakes. Jesus reminds us that we must offer each other the refreshing water of forgiveness. We are to live in love, even as He loved us and laid down His life for us, because this is God's Will.

Through our abbess we ask for our daily bread. This is significant. Our food is to do the Will of our Father in Heaven, and it is she who mediates to us, individually and as a community, the Will of the Lord. It is not her will that she serves to her flock, but that which is given her for us, the indication of God's Will and her very life. An abbess' life is a life consumed—her time, her prayer, her strength are wholly given.

Vespers finishes quietly, and the lights are turned off. We pray silently, together.

And then it is time for supper. As we emerge from the chapel, I glance out at the garth retreating into the shadows of evening. The chickadees and juncos that found a winter oasis at Sr. Claire's feeder (with hawthorn berries for dessert) have long since gone to evergreen bivouacs, and sleep under the puffed quilts of their own feathers. There is only a duned desert of snow out there, under the first stars. The enticing aroma of the bread Sr. Maureen and Sr. Joanna baked this morning grows stronger as we approach the refectory. And there it is, brimming out of the serving pans on carts between the tables—beautiful loaves of whole wheat and white, cut in generous slices, and a mound of creamy whipped cheese. The two sisters assigned to serve stand like angels in white aprons beside the steaming jugs of cocoa. My spirit fed, my body now asks earthly nourishment in healthy hunger. And well is it satisfied. Our desert has the most delicious manna!

VIII

YES, FATHER!

(March)

It's already Passion Week—early this year. The sun is warm in an almost clear sky; the first signs of spring play on my winter-starved senses. The snow has just about disappeared, at least for the moment, and the first snowdrops are in full bloom—delicate white blossoms that look vulnerable to the slightest storm. (This is an illusion. They are really very hardy and endure all kinds of weather unscathed.) Today their petals are flung wide, and the three little green hearts on their corollas are in plain view. Nothing else has blossomed yet, except a few daring crocuses, though there are green noses poking up wherever there is a hyacinth or a daffodil bulb waking from winter sleep. I have a crocus and a couple of clumps of daffodils planted to each side of the shoe shop door, and I check each day on their progress. But nothing can beat the lowly snowdrops in quick response to the sun. They nod on their fragile stems two inches above the soil, with their narrow leaves making upright exclamation points: yes, yes, yes!

I've come to love the word *yes*. It's short and simple, but it says everything that is in my heart. It's the shortest of prayers. For me, it sums up the way to God that Jesus followed Himself and as understood and taught by Saint Benedict in his Rule. That way is the way of an obedience that is mature, willed, yet as simple as the snowdrop. But even for Jesus it wasn't always easy.

I have our abbess' shoes to repair today. I want to do the best job I can, but it looks like it will be something of a challenge.

Well-fitting shoes are important, poor repairs can do damage to feet! Though it is secondary I want to make them look nice as well as feel comfortable, and this pair has seen plenty of service— service to the community day in and day out. They need new elastic over the instep, and the rubber wedges on the heels need to be replaced. The uppers call for a bit of stitching, too, here and there. My examination completed, I begin the job of removing the old elastic.

What makes the abbess special? Well of course she is charged with responsibility for all the business of the monastery, for the way of life, for each sister, for the seeking of God's Will for the community. There is a wonderful mystery in her relationship to her community as a whole, and within that mystery, that of her relationship to each of the sisters. The mystery concerns the presence of Christ inspiring her and even acting through her. In wonder we notice how effectively He gives her that special grace for the direction of the community and for each sister. All this is true in virtue of her office, regardless of her human weaknesses, and/ or those of the rest of us. It is a matter of faith from both viewpoints, though sometimes it may ask a lot of us, as in the case of an assignment that seems beyond our strength. Saint Benedict took that possibility in hand himself in chapter 68 of his Rule, making it clear that we may present our difficulties to the abbess. This presumes one has really tried first. It is called "dialogued obedience," to be carefully distinguished from argument. Actually it is a good opportunity for growth in understanding for both participants.

I'm not sure I can fix up these old shoes. Maybe they will be bad for her feet. Maybe it is a waste of time and material . . . or . . . might it be that it is a lot of work and I have other things I'd planned to do? Or I might do a bad job and be ashamed? If I listen to that, I am losing an opportunity to live my vow of obedience in a small way, a way that no one would pick up but God, who has shown me so clearly the love of Christ as most totally expressed in obedience. By the time I get my thought back on the positive line I am already through sewing the new elastic into place with my sewing awl, a handy little tool, and I test the elasticity with my hand to see that it will hold firm without binding.

Now on to the rubber heels: good rubber heels help us to walk quietly, and can save the wearer from slipping, but like everything else they do wear down. I remove the rubber and smooth the bottoms of the hard heels on the big noisy lathe, select two new rubber heel pads and apply glue.

The shoe shop darkens. The sun that was pouring in the barn view windows when I came has hidden behind sudden clouds. Winter still has power to return. I can't see well enough to stitch Mother's shoes, so I get up and switch on the light. Does that dark sky hold more snow? If it does, the poor little green noses will get nipped and the brave crocuses will be squashed. But the supple snowdrops will come through unharmed. Sometimes they get buried in snow for as long as a couple of weeks, but it doesn't seem to put so much as a crimp in their leaves.

My thoughts move on, still reflecting on our vow of obedience. Sometimes it is harder to maintain yes in its full positivity in our relations with one another in the community. It is so easy to slide into interior griping, which quickly messes up one's life of love and prayer. Habitual griping is a "no" that builds a prison. But a mistaken understanding of obedience can also build a prison. True obedience is a free yes, with the emphasis on freedom. I remember something that happened when I was on retreat for first vows. I was out for a walk, and at the top of a gentle descent in the road, and I was thinking about how I was binding myself hand and foot to be offered to God. At that moment I was flooded with a sense of freedom that became awe, so different from anything I had ever experienced. I said to myself, I never knew this existed—it is so far beyond what I had understood as freedom. Of course this high point didn't stay in my full consciousness, but I have never forgotten it, and its effect remains.

The Mount of Olives, the Mount of Calvary held the summits of Jesus' Passion, and in both there was darkness and a journey. Going through the dark, trusting in God, draws me powerfully. There is a passage in Isaiah that expresses the challenge of faith in a very striking way. "Who among you fears the Lord, heeds His servant's voice, and walks in darkness without any light, trusting in the name of the Lord and relying on his God? All of you kindle flames and carry about you fiery darts; walk by the light of your own fire and by the flares you have burnt!"* Whenever this passage comes to mind, I'm eager to walk through that darkness without any light but Jesus. I want to say an unconditional *yes*, trusting in my Father. The pathos of the second sentence fills me with sorrowful recognition. It is hard to keep the same serene faith in God's love and providence when things go wrong, when I trip on unseen jagged rocks, or hit my head on heaven knows what, and nothing makes any sense. This is the testing point. In panic, out come the matches to scratch up a flare of worldly prudence. Something must be wrong somewhere. But it's not. The directions are: throw away the matches. If you can't go forward in faith in monastic life, forget it. Try some other ascent.

If God invites us to walk in darkness of faith in a radical way, He does not leave us without the guidance we need. It comes through another sense—hearing. The servant's voice reaches us in the gloom. Who is the servant? Isaiah? Yes. Jesus? Yes. My abbess? Yes. "Listen, my child . . ." Saint Benedict begins, "receive willingly and carry out effectively your loving father's advice, that by the labor of obedience you may return to Him from whom you had departed by the sloth of disobedience." This doesn't mean that I throw away my adult mind—in fact the yes of Jesus was toweringly adult. This is where *yes* comes in: to say *yes*, to pray *yes*, to live *yes* is to walk the narrow way safely, even in the dark.

I have to admit, I don't always do that well. The way of obedience is contrary to ways of thinking and acting that are so thoroughly entrenched in me that I tend to identify with them. Obedience can feel like obliteration, but it is only self-centeredness that suffers. It makes us God-centered. Childishness is pitiable in an adult, and abdication of responsibility is despicable, but true Christian obedience is the crown of human development. The world and the devil tried to obliterate Jesus on Calvary. They could not. By His *yes* Jesus turned the tables, obliterating death. He trusted right through all.

My best *yes* is all full of holes, but even the holes have a purpose. A solid shoe is an ornament. A shoe without the hole that is

* Isa 50:10-11.

space for a living foot would never walk anywhere. A snowdrop without tubules to conduct the sap that sustains life would never live to nod in the sun. If Jesus' *yes* did not fill my *yes*, if any positive response I manage to make was not subsumed in His perfect response, it would be of no value whatsoever. Jesus *is* response to the Father. This teaches me an optimism no failure can eradicate.

Jesus lived His *Amen, Abba!* so completely, so thoroughly, so perfectly that He fulfilled it. He identified with it. He *is* the response of *Yes, Father!* He fills *yes* to its farthest corners. There is no part of *yes*, no *yes* anywhere that He did not reach in His *yes* on the cross. Therefore, to the extent that I enter into *Yes, Father*, it is no longer I, but He in me, that lives unto God.

"Christ became obedient for us even unto death, dying on the cross . . ."* (as in the traditional Cistercian responsory for Good Friday). He took His *yes*, the *Yes* that He is, down to the roots of the great *no* of death, down to the consequences of every *no* any man has said or lived from the beginning of the world. But what *no* has any being? *No* is precisely lack of being, refusal to be. Jesus took His *yes* down into death by dying in it and being fixed in it—arms spread wide, Heart open. But how could nonbeing hold Being? How could *no* swallow *yes?* How could death extinguish Him who *is* Life? And so, having touched bottom, He began His ascent, drawing with Him all the partial *yeses* that had been held in death, because all *yeses* are His *yes*.

The power-wave of His Rising has not abated. It reaches from end to end of time and space. We of the weak and stumbling ascents are drawn upward into that movement more and more strongly. We follow the Servant up the mountain of God, through the narrow ravine, through the caverns that paradoxically seem to go down, deeper and deeper into its heart. We know in faith this darkness leads to greater revelation than Tabor; we know this way breaks out on the summit of love.

I look around the shoe shop, I look at the boots and shoes waiting for mending, I look down at the shoe in my hand: old shoes, worn beautiful: Christ's shoes. Yes, especially the shoes I'm

* Phil 2:7-9.

mending today are Christ's shoes. The abbess holds the place of Christ in the monastery; not an easy role, and He works through her in a special way when both we and she have faith in Christ and in each other. We must have faith to follow her, true, but more is asked of her. She must have faith to accept her role in the face of her own weaknesses, to believe in the mystery of Christ in herself for others. She must dare to be what she is called to be; and that is continuously humbling. She must lead through the underground ascent, "exhorting, entreating, rebuking" and trusting beyond anything that is asked of the rest of us. Jesus says to her, "She who hears you hears Me, and she who hears Me, hears Him who sent Me." By a special light within the grace that goes with her office, she is enabled to touch each one of us wherever we are within the mountain. In the really difficult spots, she reaches us her hand, steadies us by her voice, and warns us of sheer drops to right or left. There've been many tough spots for me, especially in the beginning. There were places I had to crawl through endlessly on hands and knees, leaving a bit of my skin behind, and horrible chimneys to climb. I remember the one that was so narrow I had to abandon my back pack that I thought held the essentials for my survival. In all these I was helped, humanly, strongly, but also divinely. I don't know what lies ahead, but is it any wonder I should trust?

I put Mother's finished shoes in my basket and take up another mending job. These are disciple's shoes; big hulking barn boots for a child . . . of God. Maybe the idea of being a child doesn't appeal to the modern world. Maybe it never appealed too strongly at any time in history. We're a proud race. Even Jesus' immediate disciples, the Chosen Twelve, had a hard time swallowing this business of "unless you turn, and become a child again. . . ." But it is of the essence of our relationship with our Heavenly Father to receive all from Him; to give all back to Him in love, to be caught up in the Divine relationship. Isn't this the keynote of Sacred Scripture from the creation accounts of Genesis to the new heavens and new earth of Revelation 21? "I will be your God, you will be my people" is a leitmotif of the Old Testament. The Psalms are familiar witnesses of the Israelites' sense of kinship with God even when they are cries of pain, anger or

bewilderment. But the New Testament shows us Jesus above all
as the child of the Father, the Son. He teaches us what it means
to be son, and why suffering is necessary for love to reach full
expansion—or He will if we will let the knowledge in. "Incline
the ear of your heart," Saint Benedict directs.

How grateful I am for the inspired translation of all this into
the way of obedience in the monastery! I have a Rule that has
guided the growth of countless holy men and women over the
centuries. I have the Cistercian Fathers in their writings, and the
contemporary example of my brothers and sisters in the Order,
especially those I live with. I have my abbess, whose role is not
arbitrary or outworn. It is of the essence of the Benedictine-
Cistercian way. This does not mean my surrender is not directly
to the Father, but it means I have a way of living it out, concretely,
in every detail of my life. It means I have the help I need to know
what God is asking.

The monastic vocation is a call that elicits a radical response,
and it continues so to the end. It is a call to put on the mind of
Christ, to enter into His Heart, a call to give everything in response
to the Father's love. Everything has been delivered to Jesus by
the Father, and no one knows the Father but the Son and those to
whom the Son reveals Him. Jesus reveals Him to the little ones,
the poor ones, the ones who come to Him freely and put their
necks under His yoke: sonship. It is indeed sweet and light. It
only takes a loving surrender in faith of that "adult" self that
wants to rely solely on itself, and thus be its own father. The ways
of grace to this end are many but everyone is called to it. Without
becoming a child again, no one enters the Kingdom. For me, it's
very concrete. I'm called to journey under a Rule and an abbess.
The disciple's boots go beside the master's shoes in my basket.

A ray of sun slants through a rift in the clouds as I leave the
shoe shop. It falls directly on the little trembling snowdrops, like
a pointing finger, accenting their whiteness. They've grown their
journey through dark earth, called by the warmth of the sun,
before they broke out into pure light. I stop for a long look, and
let my heart take its cue. Yes, Father! *Amen, Abba!* And I dare to
pray it in union with Jesus' whole Heart.

IX

THEN FACE TO FACE

(April)

The first streaks of sunset call me, as I wash my dishes after supper. Through the kitchen windows I see that the clouds that bar the western sky are beginning to glow peachy-gold behind Saint Patrick's Hill. Quickly I return the clean dishes, and make my way by the shortest route through the house and out to the road that leads to the barn. It's one of the best places to watch the sunset.

It is really developing into a spectacular sky full of color. Peachy-gold has deepened to rose—rippled all over the western sky in shadings and brightnesses. I lean against a tree trunk, and look. The sun, four times its normally perceived size, has escaped from the cloud bank now, slipping down swiftly over the rim of the world. I can see it going—bright orange behind the black fili-gree of April trees in bud.

Rose becomes red: glowing like coals under a bellows. I leave my tree, and walk down the road under the bannered sky. I find myself at the end of the forsythia hedge when I stop. A red shine catches the corner of my eye. It is sunset reflected in the attic window over the shoe shop. The attic window frame is coming out. The wood is too rotten to hold it any more. I regard the old Shops Building affectionately, and just a little sadly. Poor old thing, with its wavering walls and crooked chimney, its time has almost come. This is its last spring. It is to be replaced by a new building with concrete floors and straight walls. The little gray stove will yield to efficient central heating. The plans are already being drawn, and each one of us who works in the employments involved has a share in the plans for her new place—where to

49

put windows, where to locate electrical outlets and so on. It's fun. I've drawn a plan of the new shoe shop on graph paper, and move bits of paper proportionally representing the lathe and other equipment around, and dream, especially of windows. The new place will have big, back windows looking out over the field toward the edge of the woods. But even in the face of that, and the knowledge that the old place needs to go before it falls down on our heads, I feel a pang for an old friend.

The sunset has gone down to embers now. I turn, and walk slowly back toward the house in the growing dusk. I glance toward the cemetery as I round the corner by the chapter room.* The cemetery isn't a frightful place in the monastery, or even a mournful one. It's a dear place—part of the setting of our life—accepted as simply as refectory or chapter room or Church. There have been only two deaths in the community since its foundation in 1949.** The first sister died in 1950, well before I entered. The other sister's death occurred in 1974. I knew Sr. Patricia very well, from her entrance into the community to her death. Her final days and her Pasch are a memory none of those here at the time will forget. A death in the monastic context is quite a different experience from a death in other milieus. We are deeply attached to our sisters in religion, but the natural sadness of seeing them no more is combined with such joy for them, and so great a sense of communion with them in Christ, that we are lifted up rather than cast down by their passing. Sr. Pat died of cancer, after a protracted illness lasting several months. We watched her body waste away, and saw the beautiful work the Lord was accomplishing in her become more and more manifest. We saw the last mighty leaps of spiritual growth. We enjoyed her nurses' accounts of her flashes of humor, and suffered with her through her struggle. On the morning of December 2, as Reverend Mother was leaving Sr. Pat's room, she heard a whisper from the bed, "Jesus, I'm ready." Again, more firmly, "Jesus, I'm ready." Then, shortly after noon, after a

---

* The "chapter room" is the place where the community assembles for talks and discussions, and where regularly a *chapter* of the Rule of Saint Benedict is read aloud, hence the name.

** Statistics at the time of writing.

brief agony she died. I remember the bells ringing, and all of us going to the infirmary. I remember Sr. Pat's hands, lying gently open across her waist in a gesture of peace and grace. It was an unseasonably mild day and I have the impression the window was open and a bird sang. I know the sun smiled like spring. It beamed through the window on that ravaged face, and on Reverend Mother's hand, holding Sr. Pat's chin in place until rigor mortis would remove the need. Instead of feeling solemn and sad, there was a lighthearted spirit moving among us. Strained faces in the corridor gave way to smiles. Sr. Pat had been set free. We had the impression she was dancing among us, laughing like a child—and soon we were laughing too, dearly, simply.

We kept watch beside her body in the chapter room. She was never left alone. We prayed the rosary and the Psalter. The Psalms had new meaning. I remember especially Psalm 84. Ever since that day, whenever I pray that Psalm, I think of Jesus coming for Sr. Pat. "Faithfulness and mercy have met; justice and peace have embraced. . . ."

The abbot of Spencer and a carload of monks joined us for the funeral. After the Mass, we took Sr. Pat's body to the cemetery, and laid it to rest next to that of Mother Saint John. And then we went back into the cloister—and again that lighthearted spirit danced among us, irresistibly. Sr. Pat's own mother was there for the funeral, and came into the cloister afterwards. She felt it too, and started remembering funny things about her Mary Anna, and chuckling. Her delicious laugh was contagious, and soon we were all laughing. A diocesan priest, here on retreat at the time, was present too. After a bit, the monks and the priest and "Mama Freda" left. Someone making a visit in the chapel whispered to the priest, "Say, what's going on in there?" His reply was, "You'd *never guess!*"

I salute Sr. Pat's and M. Saint John's graves from the distance in passing, and go in the back door, headed for chapel with sunset in my heart. I stop to take one last look through the cloister window. The clouds are gray now, with only a dusty blush on their undersides. Soon it will be night.

My own attitude toward death has gone through several stages. When I was a small child, death wasn't very real. It touched other people, not me. When I was nine, my sister's accidental death changed that irrevocably. My beautiful, vivacious, middle sister was gone, and because we had been very close, I was shattered. At the same time, my faith in God was tempered—like steel—by her faith in accepting death. The next stage was a terrible struggle to come to terms with the fact that some day I, too, would have to die. I knew it was so intellectually, but psychologically I couldn't confront the fact. I'm ashamed to say this lasted until several years after I entered the monastery. One Good Friday I finally faced it. I made my surrender, telling Jesus that I accept my death, whenever, wherever, however He wills it. Great and lasting peace ensued. I still dread the process of dying, the failing of my systems and faculties, the pain . . . but I no longer fear the fact.

The thought of death is useful, rather than morbid. It puts life in perspective, and helps me recognize what is really important and what trivial. If I were to die tonight, would this little misunderstanding have the space of two seconds of my precious attention? Or would that matter I have to attend to be allowed to steal the chance I have to smile at my sister in Christ just once more? And would I do or say that other thing if I knew I'd have to render an account tonight? How would I live today if I knew this sunset was the last these eyes would see? I think I'd want to live it simply, just as usual—but with enormous love and gratitude.

The chapel is lovely in evening shadow. There are many of my sisters praying quietly here and there, but though together, each one of us is alone.

Lord, I look forward to the sunset of my life. Sunset in one place is sunrise in another. You know how my spirit tugs sometimes, and how, O Morning Star, I long to see Your face! What will death be like from the *inside*? Outwardly the reality will be that of a heart attack, or an accident or whatever. But what will be the inner reality? In that house of my prayer, in my mind there is a sort of window, opposite the door I use. It looks out of myself. It's night out there. My lamp is rather stubborn. Sometimes I can't get it to dim down at all, and all I see is my reflection in the window's glass, or by a change of focus, the glass itself. But to the degree I succeed in dimming my lamp, I can see out. When You will to draw aside the clouds, and let the moon and stars shine clearly, then I see—as one sees in the night—a country there, more beautiful than I can say. Once, when gazing out, I felt my cheek caressed by a gentle dawn breeze, redolent of spring and realized the window was open. My spirit leapt, but in the very moment of that realization, the barrier of glass was there again. Perhaps . . . perhaps, death is the window becoming an open door, and Your call from the other side to let go, to trust, to come. And I will go through that different, unfamiliar door eagerly—the door that is not less, but more.

And what then? You. You forever.

You've given me so many wonderful people to love in this life—each dear in a way all his or her own. I've loved their faces and their characters, their little mannerisms and their turns of speech. Many are with You now, and all will be some day. But when You call me into the dawn, through the window-door, I know I will not find You *and* them . . . but them in You. Everything, everyone, unveiled. Everywhere I look, anyone my heart embraces, and it will be You. All their dearnesses I knew will be there, none lost—familiar, lovable ways my eyes were starved to see again—this one's quiet smile, that one's enthusiastic spirit. They are all Yours—a million dearnesses, all different, yet all Yours, and one in You. That's why I know I'll recognize You, though I've never even dreamed Your face. I'll know in an instant Yours is the countenance I've been glimpsing through a thousand human lenses all my life.

X

BETWEEN THEN AND NOW
AND FOREVER

We possess the prophetic message that is altogether reliable. You will do well to be attentive to it, as to a lamp shining in a dark place, until day dawns and the morning star rises in your hearts. (2 Pet 1:19)

Suddenly, looking around, they no longer saw anyone but Jesus alone with them. (Mark 9:9)

These two scriptural quotations give us the other side of the Transfiguration—the side which is more or less of a night journey, in that the glory is hidden under the veil of the ordinary. This is the way most of our life is lived in the monastery, which is *by choice* "ordinary, obscure and laborious."* This, however, isn't the end of Saint Bernard's description of the Cistercian vocation. It is also "joy in the Holy Spirit." What is the attraction of such a call? I believe it is the secret joy of the heart that knows it is turned to God and experiences His love and care, though it be as a blind person knows the sun by the warmth on his or her face. There is for me a special joy in answering "Here I am!" when the Lord asks: "Who is there who will walk in darkness without any light, trusting in the name of the Lord, and relying on his God?" I have come to prefer the ordinary, the obscure. I have come to love the night as somehow truer. The lights and glories of this world, even the spiritual ones, are so easily misleading, so subject to distortion by our weak senses.

* Cistercian Order of the Strict Observance, *Constitutions and Statutes* (Rome, 1990), Constitution 5.

Our journey is by nights. We are not left in total darkness, though. We have the prophetic word. We have the Gospels, in which Jesus lives and gives us light and grace by His spirit, in which He continues to reveal the Father. We are called not only to ponder and experience the prophetic message and the presence of the Lord in His Word, but also to bear it to others, to hold up the lamp for others by the way we live and love in community. We know this doesn't happen automatically. It is an ascesis of ongoing attention—to attend to the prophetic message in everything that happens, everyone we meet, in the unfolding of our own lives. *Lectio* will not bear fruit until we give it room to spread out its branches throughout our day, not closing the book as something finished, but carrying it open in our memories.

We want to see Jesus. It is really wonderful to lift up our eyes and see only Jesus. But, in the context of Mark 9, remember this means seeing Jesus in His ordinary form, without the glory, without radiant companions from the holy dead. It is to return to the state of wondering what he meant by "rising from the dead." Obviously, it didn't occur to them that He meant it literally. He wanted them to know for the future, when all was fulfilled, that this was all the divine plan, known to Him and embraced. He wanted them to have an anchor, even though they could not see or understand it. They were about to see the weakness of humanity in Jesus, in His agony in the garden, His arrest and the abuse that followed, in His condemnation and crucifixion. They needed that lamp in a dark place, that prophetic word the Father spoke to their frightened ears, "This is my Son, my beloved, in whom I am well pleased. Listen to Him."* That is enough. Enough for a lifetime.

Saint Peter is encouraging. We have his word, and the Lord's through him, that eternity will dawn for us; the bright morning star will rise in our hearts. The bright morning star, the rising sun, is a name of Jesus—Jesus revealed and revealing all. Some day we will see. Some day there will be no more questions, but only the great Answer, question and answer making completion.

* Matthew 17:5.

Here is a secret—eternity is already dawning, as a plant is already growing within the seed planted in the earth. The seed is in darkness, but the life within it pushes and swells against its barriers. Do you feel the pushing and swelling of God in your heart? Will you let go all that keeps it confined, even though you must die to your old form in order to become what the Father created you to become, *who* the Father called you into being to become? Will you let the hidden sun pull you out of your shell to share the life in you with others?

The best way to encourage and help others is to be faithful to our own call to listen, to embrace with joy and faith the presence of the Lord in them with the love of the Holy Spirit which is poured out in our hearts.

FAMILY, SCHOOL, AND CALL:
A RETROSPECTIVE

When I think of my life from early childhood to my eighth birthday, my memories are full of brightness, for it was a golden time in my life. I was the third and last child to be born to my parents. My two sisters were quite a bit older than I. After the birth of Agnes, the second child, the doctor told Mother that she must have no more children, since she had been in great danger giving birth (she was in labor four days) and almost lost her baby as well as her own life. But as the years went on Mother longed for one more, and I guess Dad did too.

Of course they would have been delighted if I had been twin boys to round out the family, but I was welcomed with love and joy. This happy event occurred by caesarean section on May 24, 1933, in Baguio, Benguet, Luzon, Philippines. I was given the name Sarah Alice Day, though my family and friends always called me Sally. My grandmother, Nanon Leas Worcester, had her home in Baguio. From the hospital my mother brought me there to spend my first days in the world, welcoming the air I first breathed, cool and sweet with the scent of pine trees, unknown in the lowlands, and smoke. As I learned a few years later the smoke was usually from the outdoor housekeeping of an interesting people called Igarotes, who were one of several groups native to the region and different in origin from the lowland Filipinos. One of my family's teasing nicknames for me was "Igarote Sal."

You are probably wondering why we were living in the Philippines. My grandfather, Dean Conant Worcester, was invited to go to the Philippines in 1900, shortly after the end of the Spanish-American War, when the Philippine Islands became a protectorate of the USA. He was to assist in the government to be set up for the country. He agreed, and with his wife Nanon and their two children, Alice Electa, age 4, and Frederick Leas, age 2, made the long journey from Ann Arbor, Michigan, to Manila, and settled in. The family liked the Philippines.

The story of the years that followed is too long to tell here, but my grandparents lived the rest of their lives there, punctuated by occasional trips back to the USA for short visits, and both died in the Philippines. Although they belonged to no church and their children were not baptized, their ashes were saved under grave tiles in the Episcopalian Cathedral in Manila, a building that was destroyed during World War II. Their son was able to recover the ashes of Dean and Nanon Worcester, and they were brought back to the USA and buried in our family gravesite in Vermont. Their children, too, spent most of their lives in the Philippines, though neither died there.

The D. C. Worcester family went through various homes. At some point Dean discovered a small town in the mountains. He chose to build a house there, though Baguio was quite simple and undeveloped. He loved the wildness of the area, and was very interested in the bird and animal wildlife. More than that, he was interested in the people and made friends even with the headhunters who lived in groups in the mountains, risking his life to help them find better conditions for living. He died nine years before I was born, in the act of trying to help a friend who had come to visit him in the hospital, got very excited about what he was sharing, and fainted. Grandfather got out of bed, picked him up, put him on the bed, and immediately dropped dead himself from an aneurysm.

"Nana," as we called our grandmother, was the only grandparent I knew, and she was precious. One interesting story about her was that at some point in her life she had contracted tuberculosis, and recovered from it completely by living outdoors for a year, on a porch, in Baguio's clean air. At the time there was no other treatment available for the dread disease. Baguio is now much developed and well known as a holiday spot.

Back to 1933: when my mother was well enough again, she brought me home. Our home was in the outskirts of Manila. It was in Manila that I was baptized as a baby in the Anglican Cathedral of Saint Mary and Saint John. My next-older sister, Agnes Elizabeth, was 9 years old at the time, and took special interest in her baby sister. Our oldest sister, Anne, was 14. I don't remember many things about Anne during this prewar time, probably because she was away at a boarding school in the USA for a good part of my first 6 years. The one thing I do remember (when I was 5 or 6) is her white horse, Snowdon. Anne let me ride him at a walk on the beach, and I loved that. The other thing I remember was her singing. She loved to sing and played the piano to accompany herself.

Agnes took care of me as often as she was able. She had lots and lots of friends, and when they came to our house in Manila to visit, she not only let me stay with the group but encouraged my presence. She taught me how to swim at a very young age— before I could walk, I think! Then she saved my life one day when I was playing in the middle of a dirt road next to a peanut field, planted right in front of our property. A car was coming and I didn't pay attention to her cry to me. She bravely lunged out from the edge of the road to grab my arm and jerked me out of danger just in time. Was I grateful? No! I was mad at her for several days because she hurt my arm! She understood and didn't love me any less.

I started kindergarten at the American School and made new friends, and then continued there into first grade. One day I was surprised by a great discovery. As was often the case, I was casually looking at pictures in the books on the bookshelves in my room, which were full of my sisters' outgrown literature. I looked at the letters, and suddenly began to recognize words. It dawned on me that now I could read the stories! From that day on I was a book fiend, reading everything I could get my hands on.

Another memory at about the same time was a tragedy. Right next to our house was another lovely house belonging to cousins of ours. There was a grandmother named Helen, her daughter called little Helen, with the latter's husband and three children, one of whom was also named Helen. One day my sister Agnes and I went with the mother Helen and her three children for a swim in a public pool. The next day we all got sick. Helen and the oldest child, her stepdaughter Janie, died in the hospital from polio. The two youngest children, Helen the fourth and her little brother Wade, were badly crippled. I don't remember this clearly as I was very sick, too, and as I was told later so was Agnes, but neither of us was crippled by the experience.

Unable to bear this tragedy, which came on top of his first wife's death and only a few years into his new marriage, the children's father left home and joined the US Army. When the two crippled children were well enough to travel, their grandmother took them to the USA for them to recover their ability to walk. A play hut and a small desk that had been Janie's were passed on to me, and I wondered very much about the whole experience.

I have memories of going to church with my mother. After the service we went out for breakfast—a big treat. Maybe other family members went to church, too, but I don't remember that. Mother took on a job of teaching the children the beginnings of their faith. We read the Bible together, and acted out Bible stories in a large sand box. The one that is clear in my mind was the story of Joseph and his coat of many colors. I felt very bad about the brothers who sold Joseph and took his beautiful coat and ripped it and put animal blood on it and took it to their father, whose heart was torn with sorrow as he imagined Joseph had been killed by some beast.

At home Agnes played with me and told me stories. When I was about six years old she started teaching me to cook. Dad said that when I could put a whole dinner on the table, including a good cup of coffee, he would give me a prize. Standing at the stove on a box with Agnes advising me, I finally managed to reach that momentous accomplishment when I was seven and in the States.

There was a family practice we observed: returning to the USA every five years to visit family there. I went the first time when I was two years old. Naturally, I have no memory of the visit, though I've heard plenty of stories. At this time my parents bought a lovely old brick house in Orford, New Hampshire, to have a real home base in the USA. The second trip was in 1940.

The whole family went, except for Anne who chose to stay behind. During the voyage Mother received a cable from her brother that her mother had died. I remember that so clearly because Nana was much loved by all of us.

What struck me most was that Mother didn't cry. I knew she loved her mother and couldn't understand why she wasn't all in tears. Only later in my life did I learn that my Dad couldn't stand tears, probably out of his experience of a boyhood in a strict family. My father's parents had both died some time before he married my mother. I knew very little about his childhood and family until World War II, when I lived with one of his sisters and two generations of her family. I don't know why he decided to come to the Philippines, which he did as a young man, after graduating from Harvard and then from a business college in New York.

Another happening on the ship was that I had my seventh birthday. We landed in Hawaii on the way, and I was able to spend a day with a family I had known in Manila in kindergarten and first grade at the American School. Their oldest boy, Sonny, was a special friend of mine, to the amusement of both of our families. (His real name was Robert, after his father.)

We continued with our voyage the next day, and landed in San Francisco. While we were there we went to visit the famous Mount Shasta. I was told there was real snow on top of this wonderful mountain. I was very excited, especially about the snow, because I secretly thought snow was the source of the world's supply of white sugar, the sugar my Dad used to put in his morning coffee without stirring it so I could scrape out the coffee sugar to eat when he was finished. I got my secret idea from the white shiny stuff I'd seen on Christmas cards. The car went up the winding road, and soon we saw the snow. When we finally stopped I jumped out into some very dirty snow and took a double handful of it to stuff into my mouth. The result was my first great disillusionment!

While in California, we also went to the World's Fair in San Francisco. My only surviving memory was of falling asleep after walking and walking and gawking, and waking up to find my Dad carrying me. And we visited the Redwoods forest, looking in wonder at those fantastically huge trees. Then I think we went by train across the country, to Orford, New Hampshire, where our brick house waited for us.

We spent a happy summer there, in the lovely house with its "ice box" and fireplaces and curving staircase. The property ran down to the Connecticut River, looking across to Vermont. I do have many memories of that summer. One was that Sonny Gordon was sent up to us by train for a visit, with his name and destination on a sign he wore around his neck. His family was also taking a USA break!

When it was time to return to the Philippines my parents were informed that neither Agnes nor I would be allowed to go, because of the disturbed conditions in the Far East. Dad had to go, because he was needed at the Philippine Refining Company, his workplace. He went alone, Agnes went off to a Massachusetts boarding school where she would finish her senior year in high school, Mother and I stayed in Orford, and I went to the local school when it opened in the fall. It was a wonderful feeling for me to go off to school walking through fall leaves and later snow, carrying my lunch bag like the American-born children. There were four grades in a room in Orford's public school at the time. Because I could already read, I was put in third grade, something I was sorry about later because the beginnings of math and learning to tell time were taught in the second grade, both things I needed to learn. But I did have a good time and made lots of new friends. When Agnes came back for Christmas vacation, we made snowmen, and angels in the snow for the first time, assisted by Mother who had spent a few winters in the USA when she was young. Later, we received the news that Anne was to be married, and was unwilling to wait. So father was the only one of the family to be present for the wedding.

Winter ended and spring came and I had my eighth birthday. Spring turned into summer, a good time for fishing and swimming and long walks. In the fall, Mother received a letter from Dad begging her to come back to the Philippines, and proposing that she leave me with one of his sisters who lived in Bryn Mawr, Pennsylvania. Agnes could take care of herself at the University of Michigan, where she was enrolled.

Mother acquiesced, bought her ticket and made the arrangements. She was due to return to us in the USA on December 8, in good time for Christmas. She took me to Bryn Mawr, and introduced me to Aunt Mary, her daughter Miranda and Miranda's husband "Dizzy" (Francis Allan Bartow), and their two children, "Peter" (Francis Allan Bartow, Jr.) and "Jay" (Josiah Blackwell). Peter was 3 years older than me, and Jay 4 years younger. I had never met them before. Mother, Aunt Mary, and I went to visit the school I would be attending, a short walk away. I was told I was too young to go into fourth grade, and would be in third (again!). The next morning Mother said goodbye and was off to the Philippines.

It was a considerable change for me, to say the least. After a few days there, I was assigned to keep an eye on little Jay. I did my best to lose him—he was too young to be a playmate. I had much, much to learn. In time, I became almost a family member with the Bartows. My first year at the school chosen for me was good. I started learning French, and struggled with math. I made new friends. We were supposed to take a nap on the second-storey porch at a break time. One day as I was folding my blanket using the railing to help me, someone came up behind me and pushed my head down. I bit the railing and the result was a broken front tooth! Well, Mother would be back for Christmas.

Suddenly, on December 7, there was terrible news: the surprise bombing of the many U.S. Navy ships at port in Pearl Harbor, Oahu, Hawaii, by the Japanese. Many people were killed, many ships were sunk. The President, Franklin D. Roosevelt, declared war on Japan. This was quickly followed by declaration of war against Adolf Hitler's Germany and we were into World War II. The conquest of the Philippines did not last long: the bombings were closely followed by an army of Japanese soldiers. In time we received news through the Red Cross that Mother, Dad, Anne and her husband had been rounded up, and taken to Santo Tomás Internment Camp, a takeover from a very large college belonging to the Jesuits. Americans were considered to be "enemy aliens," though not so members of the US military. I wondered if I would ever see my family again.

My comfort was Agnes—we kept in touch by letters. She suggested to Aunt Mary that it would be good for both of us if I could be sent out to Ann Arbor, Michigan, for the summer, since she and a college friend were going to have a big house to guard for some wealthy people who were going away for the summer. I was told I could go, and I went with joy. It was a summer I'll always remember. I liked Agnes' classmate who was sharing the house with us. While I was there I met C. Mark Gilson, who was dating my sister. He was in the Navy, finishing his course in dentistry. I liked him right away, and was so happy for and with my sister. One day Agnes and Mark went out for a walk and got caught in a rain storm. When they arrived back I insisted they take their wet shoes off and I got them hot tea. I imagine they were amused by a nine-year-old telling them what to do, but they didn't show it.

A few memories: Agnes was a good seamstress, and made two big sister/little sister outfits for us. There was a cherry tree full of cherries in the yard. We were invited to visit Mark's home, to meet his father and brother (his mother had died), and we did so and stayed several days. The only distressing part of our summer was the continuing bad news from the war fronts. Then one evening Agnes and I talked with each other about death.

Summer came to an end, and I returned to Bryn Mawr, and began fourth grade in school. On Sundays the family went to a Presbyterian church a few blocks away from the Bartows' home. We usually walked there, and I was expected to go to the Sunday school. Privately, I didn't like this because the service wasn't like that of the Anglican Church I knew, but I was learning to keep things to myself, to stay out of trouble. I did learn a lot about the Bible, and memorized the list of the books of the Bible. I was growing into the family I was living with, except that I was Aunt Mary's special charge, and she had many corrections to make.

We received some postcards from Mother and Daddy, issued by the Red Cross. They were very short, but the important thing was the signatures. We knew they were still alive! Around Christmas I received a letter from Agnes telling me that she and Mark were going to get married, and she hoped I wouldn't feel cut off from her, because I never would be. I quickly replied that I was delighted with her news and wouldn't want her to feel she was hurting me. The time was set for late March. I was invited to be in the wedding party, in the Episcopal Church in Ann Arbor, to carry something. I learned later that the adults in the family (on both sides) tried to dissuade Agnes from such a young marriage (she was 19), and to wait for the end of the war; but the young couple were certain they wanted to go ahead. Mark would soon be on overseas duty.

The time crawled by to the spring, and I went out to Michigan to participate in the wedding. Other relatives were there, though the only one I remember being there was my aunt Elizabeth, who had married my mother's brother, but I'm sure Aunt Mary must have been there too, disapproving or not. Mark and Agnes gave me a white Bible to carry in the wedding and to keep.

After the wedding I went back to the Bartows' and back to school. Two weeks went by. I invited one of my classmates to walk home with me. I asked her to wait outside while I checked out with my cousin Miranda if I could invite her to supper. I walked into the kitchen where my temporary mother was stirring something on the stove. She looked up, and I got a shock at the expression on her face. I said, "What is the matter?" She didn't answer. "Is it Agnes . . . ?" Again, she didn't answer. I said, "Is she dead?" She finally replied, "No, but she is dying. There was a fire last night in the corridor outside of the little apartment the young couple had made their home. Mark carried Agnes out, and they are both in the hospital, though Agnes is much more badly burned over her body." I said: "I must go to her!!" She replied that it couldn't be. Aunt Mary was already on her way to Agnes. "But she's my *sister!* I HAVE to go!" The answer had to remain no.

Aunt Mary didn't get there on time, as Agnes couldn't last long with such bad burns. I held back my tears until bedtime, the shock was so great. When I was finally alone in my bed, I cried and cried. I prayed to God asking Him why He didn't take me instead of my wonderful sister. I apparently fell asleep. Then I found myself waiting in a small room. The door opened, and Agnes walked in with a burst of sunlight, looking more beautiful than ever. I jumped toward her to hug her, but she held out her hand to stop me, telling me if I hugged her she would have to go and there were things she wanted to tell me first. She spoke about her joy. She told me she didn't want me to grieve too much, that she would always love me. I couldn't hold myself back, and gave her a mighty hug, and suddenly found myself awake. I have always believed that she really did come to me that night. A few days later we received a letter from the Episcopal priest who had officiated at Mark's and Agnes' wedding. He had heard about the tragedy and went directly to the hospital to see Agnes. He said before that moment he had no idea of the strength and depth of her Christian faith. She had been quite peaceful, knowing she was dying and accepting it.

This death was the most anguishing event in my life, but also fruitful. It called me out of my childhood in religion, giving me a surety of faith in God. I kept much of my grief to myself because the family I was living with didn't really know me or understand that it is necessary to grieve and precious to remember, even if you are still a child on the outside. I looked for a mountain to climb and hide, but I had to narrow it down to climbing a tree to get a quiet space to deal with myself.

The months and years passed on, as the terrible war claimed more and more lives. I went on to the fifth grade, and then to the sixth. Peter and Jay became my brothers in many ways, and this was a really good development for all three of us. Once in a while we would receive a postcard telling us that my parents and Anne were still alive. The war in Europe came to an end on May 7, 1945, with the surrender of Germany, though there was a high cost in lives on all sides. News was coming in of MacArthur's return invasion of the Philippines. As it happened, Peter and I were both down with chicken pox and then mumps. Being sick is usually very boring, but not that time! I was given a little radio and was glued to the news as I prayed for the safety of my dear ones. The Santo Tomás Internment Camp was captured by a surprise action, and the internees were saved from the horrible death planned by the captors through that sneak attack arranged by General Douglas MacArthur toward the end of the war. And then the news came in fast from many sides.

My father recorded a message which was sent to me, telling me that they were alive and free, and would be coming as soon as they could. I received a recording of his message from some kind soul unknown to me. People all over the country were picking up messages like mine, and sending them on to the relatives. A little time went by, and there was another message that they were on their way home on a US Navy ship, landing in California. And then, the phone rang one day for me, and I heard my father's and my mother's voices on the other end. They had arrived, and were preparing to take the train to Philadelphia and the local to Bryn Mawr. I was beside myself with joy.

We went to meet them at the station. I had a secret fear that I might not recognize my Dad. I don't know why. It was probably because I had seen a lot less of him than I did of my mother, because of his work. The train arrived and two much loved and longed-for people got off, and I was in their arms with an ear to ear smile and tears running down my face at the same time. They were very thin, especially my father. They said that Anne had immediately entered the US Navy Waves in California. Her marriage had fallen apart under the strain of the concentration camp. They knew about Agnes. Someone, probably Aunt Mary, had sent them a cable which they did receive, contrary to the usual policy of their captors, and the news caused them unspeakable suffering. Many years later I found a notebook diary written by my mother. She was writing out her sorrow because her husband couldn't bear speaking about it.

Mother and Dad stayed at some nearby facility, as there was not enough room in the Bartows' house for them. I saw them every day, and enjoyed celebrating my twelfth birthday with them, beginning with a cup of real coffee, which I had been promised long before, when I used to sit with them watching the sun rise over Manila Bay as they drank morning coffee. We had a lot of catching up to do. Mother had not been ready to find her little girl on the edge of becoming a teenager. Mark Gilson came to meet my parents and to tell them how sorry he was. My parents encouraged him to marry again, since he was a young man.

When my school closed for the summer, we said goodbye to the Bartows and went up to our home in Orford. Mother and Dad decided to have Agnes' body exhumed and brought to Vermont to be reburied in the family plot. There was to be a little service at the new grave. When we returned home after the service I was very tired and went to sleep. I dreamed I was searching for Agnes everywhere, and hoped she would come to me as she had before, but I hunted in vain. Following this, to make up any way I could for the sorrow we all felt, I wanted to do everything the way I thought Agnes would do it, until one day when I was alone in a downstairs room, Daddy came in and gave me a gentle hug as he said: "Sally, don't try to be Agnes. You can't be, and if you keep it up, I will have lost you both." I understood, and loved him all the more.

One morning the great news came of the surrender of Japan and the end of the war. What a relief! When fall was near, we moved to a sublet apartment in Orange, New Jersey, where I was enrolled in a girls' school just a little walk and a bus ride away from our apartment building. I made friends with a Jewish girl, who went to the same school and was in 7th grade, living in the apartment building next to ours. We would walk to the bus station together, take the bus, and come home together at the end of the school day often stopping for an ice-cream cone. Sugar was no longer rationed! I made a pet of a wounded bird we found, keeping him in our garage space. Sometime after Christmas Dad felt he was strong enough to return to the Philippines to try to piece together his business at the Philippine Refining Company in Manila. He went by plane. He worked at the old office and got things running again. He found that our home in Manila had been blown up, and nothing was left but the foundation and a few poles sticking up. The sea barrier had been broken and torn down, and a good piece of the property had washed away. He found an apartment for us and leased it. Not too long after that he became dangerously ill, and was brought back to the USA and put in a hospital in California. Mother went to be with him, and I stayed with a school friend's family. Thankfully, Dad pulled out of the illness, but realized he wasn't strong enough to jump back into everything. We went back to New Hampshire after my school closed for the summer, knowing we would return to the Philippines later in the year.

I started 8th grade at the Orford school—no longer with four grades in a room. I enjoyed it without great seriousness, because

I knew I'd be going back to school in Manila, which has a different school year to suit the climate. We were booked to go on a
freighter in December, from Seattle—the date was uncertain. We
crossed the country by train, and found a hotel in Seattle. I remember that we were high up in the hotel, and the mysterious
fog hid the ground below. I would throw bread bits to the sea
birds and delight in watching them swoop to catch them. We
went up to Canada and bought a pair of six-month-old (and full-
grown) Boxer puppies to take with us, one for Uncle Fritz's family and one for us. We named them Punch and Judy. Finally the
signal came to board the ship. It was a British commercial
freighter and heavily loaded. There were only two bunk rooms
for guests, each with two bunks, and a nice big living room with
tables and chairs. A friend of the family, also returning to Manila,
shared one room with Dad, and Mother and I took the other. The
dogs had a daytime dog house on the small deck, one up from
the main deck. At night they were brought in and put in the one
bathroom, creating disaster.

It was a wonderful trip. We ate with the crew, and as the air
grew milder played ring toss on the main deck. I made friends
with one of the engineers, who had a son at home and was making him a ship in a bottle. He also gave me a little work cleaning
the railing going down into the depths of the ship. Bets were made
on what day we would arrive in Manila. I spent a lot of time in
the fore of the ship, watching the waves and the sky, and tasting
the fresh breeze. At one point we ran into a typhoon and I had
my feet blown out behind me climbing the ladder to the upper
deck. Happily I held on with my hands, and got the feet back to
the rungs. We all gathered in the main room of our area, but the
puppy Judy didn't want to come. She was sitting on the dog house
with her ears streaming in the wind. She was dragged in for safety.
Nothing bad happened except that, in one wild roll of the ship, I
flew across the room and crashed into a post, bumping my head
hard. It gave me quite a headache and I went to lie down, which
was interpreted as being sea sick, which wasn't true and hurt my
pride! As the days went by we came into tropical waters and one
day we ran into flying fish. A good number landed on the main
deck, and we had fresh fish for dinner. Then came the thirtieth

day, when we entered the Philippine Archipelago. I sat on the floor edge of the deck, and watched and listened and sniffed. Home! We made our way through the islands to Manila Bay—but when we got closer I saw the war damage everywhere: holes in the buildings, wounded people, sad eyes.

We went to our new temporary home, an apartment which was on the second floor of a three-story building. At one end of our apartment there were outdoor stairs down to a little garden, and outside the fence around the compound was a street. I could watch the "jeepneys" go by, stuffed with people, and hear the venders calling out "Balute! Balute!" (A *balute* is a hen's egg that has been treated to make a special dish.) We settled in and soon I was back in the American School. I was happy to be back in Manila, and recognized old friends and made new ones. Our apartment was near the ocean and one day there was a flood. I looked out of a window and noticed that the parked cars looked strange, until I recognized they were partly under water. The first floor of our apartment building was flooded, but it didn't reach us.

We went to see our old house, but nothing was left of it except the cement floor. A new house was to be built, smaller than the original house, with just one floor. I don't remember how long it was before we were able to move to our own house, but I remember the joy of being close to Manila Bay, feeling the wind and listening to the lapping of the waves. My room faced the ocean. There was a nice Episcopal church to go to on Sundays, usually just Mother and me, though Dad came along sometimes. He preferred the Congregational church of his youth. He was a very sincere Christian, who lived his faith, reading his Bible every evening.

I had missed the first few weeks of school and had to be tutored on what I missed, but I was soon at home with my peers. Some of the boys and girls in my class were friends from before the War and some were new to me. Some had been in Santo Tomás with my family. The starvation diet in prison camp was especially hard on growing children, but they survived by special kindness shown to them by the older prisoners. I soon found a special girlfriend, Margaret (Margie) Alexander. Her family lived a bit farther out from Manila but she went to the American School too. Several years went by. Margie and I were both on the girls' swimming team, and on the basketball team, too. Often after school we would go to the 50-meter pool near our school to practice racing. (The American School was not just for Americans; there were many nationalities represented among the students.)

I looked forward to vacation time which always included a Baguio trip. One I remember was the time we went hiking. The mountain I mentioned at the beginning of this story was much higher than Baguio, presumably the continuation of the mountain beyond and above the city. One day Mother, Caroline Bailey—a long time school friend—and I (both of us teenagers) set out to climb to the top. It was possible to go by jeep part of the way up, so Mother hired a jeep with a driver to take us that far. As we passed caves where groups of Japanese soldiers had hidden toward the end of World War II, we shivered, for most of them died there. Caroline and her parents were prisoners at Santo Tomás with my parents. We planned to stay overnight in the guest facility on top, and arranged for the driver to return for us the next day at a set time. It was a clear, lovely day, as we started out. Caroline and I were soon in the lead, with my determined mother following a bit behind. Some of her straggling somewhat behind had to do with her looking for tree orchids, one of her personal passions (the other was birds). She was quite an expert at identification and care of the beautiful flowers. Eventually we came to a place where the trail appeared partially wiped out by a landslide. Caroline and I looked at it and at each other. We didn't want to give up, and one of us spotted footprints going across to the continuing trail, so we decided it was all right and went ahead. Mother came on the scene when we were nearly to the other side, and was quite unhappy that we had gone ahead, but she shrugged and followed. We all made it across with no mishap, and kept on going up to the top. We came to the house on top where a couple lived and received guests. One of them took us out back where there was a final rise. I climbed and gasped at the far, far-away Pacific Ocean. It was an incredible view: rice terraces spread out below on the lower levels, and all the natural beauty of wild places. We were taken back to the house where three sleeping bags were laid out for us, and a good hot supper. The next morning I returned by myself to the peak to gaze at that fantastic view, and my thoughts went back over the years.

When I was 16 we went back to the USA for a visit. I spent part of it in the hospital, where I had an appendectomy and began to have the desire to become a doctor if I could. When we went back to the Philippines a school friend who shared my interest and I followed up with working in a hospital in Baguio during our school vacation. I stayed with her and her parents as mine were away on a trip to Africa. We were permitted to take classes for nurses in training, and we were assistants in surgery as "unsterile nurses," in the delivery room, and on rounds to the patients. We even attended an autopsy. It was really a good test of whether or not we were called to medicine! At the end of our time my friend had her conclusion, which was no, and I had mine, which was yes.

We went back to Manila, and I went to stay with Marge and her family. We started our senior year in high school. Then one day I had a call from my uncle Fritz, who was responsible for me while my parents were away. There was danger of an attack by the Huckbalahop, a group of bandits. He was very uneasy about the location of the Alexanders' home far out of the city, and about his responsibility, and told me he was sending me back to the USA by plane. I packed my suitcase and said goodbye to my friends, and was off on a new adventure by myself.

Mother followed when she returned from her trip. My cousin Helen came from Florida to join us shortly after this, to live with us as her family. Her grandmother had died, and she needed a home. Her younger brother went elsewhere. Mother took Helen and me to Boston, shopping for winter clothes which neither of us had. We were to go to a boarding school in Massachusetts. Then she returned to the Philippines, after I started my senior year again at "House in the Pines School," and Helen started her sophomore year. I made friends and had a good year, though I preferred my coed school in Manila. As seniors we were applying to colleges for the next year. I applied only to Middlebury College in Vermont. Most happily, I was accepted. I only found out later that the year in a school in the States was absolutely necessary to prove my grades, and if I had not come back to the USA when I did, I would have been out of luck. Some of my Worcester relatives attended my graduation to be family for me.

Helen and I had a lovely summer in New Hampshire, more or less on our own. There was a little group of young people there that were our close friends. When the time came to go on with our schools, Helen went back to House in the Pines, and I went to Middlebury, having consulted my boyfriend's father about courses to choose. In due time my father retired from his company, and my parents returned to the USA via Jamaica, where they acquired a house for winter use, since my father couldn't tolerate the cold winter weather in New England.

In the late summer something momentous in my life happened. I took a big step when I recognized the call of Christ to become a Roman Catholic. It came about this way. My mother had become a Catholic about a year before, and my father, Helen and I used to try to argue with her about Catholicism, but she wouldn't argue. She would just walk away in order to (we presumed) pray for us. I had felt for a long time that my religious life was a mess. Mother had given me a silver rosary. I stuck it in a desk drawer and forgot about it, but something was going on in my heart. One day during my summer vacation before going back to college as a sophomore, I took the car and went to the Redemptorist church about seven miles from our home. I asked to talk to one of the priests. On the way home I kicked myself for going. It hadn't answered anything. But that night, on impulse, I got out that silver rosary and the little booklet explaining it. I sat on my bed cross-legged and following the little book, said the rosary. I slept well, and when I woke up the next morning I knew that I had crossed the line—I was a Catholic! I couldn't even remember the arguments against it that had seemed so logical in our family battle with Mother. I called the priest I had talked to the day before and told him. Then I told my mother. At first she lighted up, but her face quickly fell. "What will your father say?! He'll blame me!" I told her it was my own decision and it wasn't her fault in any way. I told her I would tell him myself. I invited him to come out for a ride with me, and I told him. He was actually quite good about it. I began taking instructions with a Redemptorist priest.

When the summer vacation was over, I went back to Middlebury for my sophomore year. I went down the hill to the Catholic Church and knocked on the door of the rectory. I asked to continue my instructions with someone there, and I was welcomed. At the end of October, on the evening before my planned big step, I went through a terrible struggle, which I believe was initiated by a devilish spirit. But the next morning, on the feast of Christ the King, I was received into the Roman Catholic Church, in the presence of my parents who surprised me by coming, despite the long drive from home, and with Ellen Hallquist, a Catholic friend from Middlebury, as my sponsor. I promptly joined the Newman Club on campus. My love for the Church grew quickly. Soon I was going to the morning Mass nearly every day.

The next two years Ellen and I were roommates. She, a cradle Catholic who had gone to Catholic schools, had to put up with my new convert enthusiasms. One day Ellen, two other college friends, and I were sitting on the floor in our dorm room playing cards. Someone told a "dirty joke," and I excused myself and left the room. Ellen really scolded me later. "What's the matter with you? Do you want to be a SAINT or something?!!" "Yes," I said, "Don't you?" What I meant was that I wanted to be with God, not to be a canonized saint. This did not go over too well with my dear friend, but worse was to come.

In my junior year in college, I was enjoying the advanced biology classes in the field of premed, since I wanted to go into the medical profession, but since Middlebury is a Liberal Arts college I was free to take some courses in other subjects. The comments of my friends on the courses given by one professor intrigued me, so for my last year I signed up for Intellectual History, a course with Professor Pardon E. Tillinghast. There was a lot about Christian ways of life in it, and it turned out to be indeed very inspiring. One assignment was to write a *critical* paper on a Christian group. I chose to write about the Cistercians, but when the paper came back to me I saw I only got a C, with the comment, "This is not critical, but appreciative!" Something was beginning to happen to me: I would find myself wondering at a wild sweetness going through me, and I began to think I was being called to become a nun. But I had no desire for that—I didn't know any and couldn't imagine myself in such a role. I had plans for other things, marriage and children and medical service. The summer following I worked for a local M.D. with my future in mind.

But the thoughts wouldn't go away and I needed help. When I was back at Middlebury I didn't want to take my anguish to a priest, because I feared being told that I was being called, but I thought of Tillinghast. I went to find him in his office, and he sat quietly, puffing at his pipe, as I told him about my inner battle, ending up with the fact that my parents would be very unhappy about such a choice, in fact it might kill my father who had serious heart problems. The answer that came was a shock. Tillinghast said it is true that we have to be sensitive to the desires and hopes our parents have for us, *except for the call of God!*

I accepted this, and recognized that I was indeed being called, but, I thought, I could still do medical work. I'll find some sisters who do medical work, and plan to join them after I graduate. I found several places where the Religious were trained in medicine to serve in medical work as their chosen field of work for God, and went to see them. They welcomed me warmly, and described their life, charism and work. They gave me books to read. I went home to think and pray, but nothing came clearly. When I went back to Middlebury for my senior year, I said to myself, "What's the matter with you? Make up your mind!!" Actually, I was quickly losing all interest in finishing college—I wanted to follow this scary path immediately, but I knew my graduation meant a lot to Dad, and it was only a matter of a few months more. At a break when I was home, I found what looked like a good book in Mother's collection, titled *The Sign of Jonas* by a Trappist monk, and started reading it. Then came a moment I'll never forget. I felt the call, not as a voice calling but in the wave of certainty I had sought in my previous visits to convents. Then I thought, they are monks and they won't take me, and I groped for understanding. When I went to Mass the next day, coming out of the Church, I told my Redemptorist pastor with a chuckle, "I've found out what I'm supposed to do—join the Trappist Monks in Gethsemani! But they won't take a woman!" He answered, "There's a new monastery for Cistercian nuns down near Boston!" "OH!" I said, overcome with wonder. He went inside, and came out with the name and address of Mount Saint Mary's Abbey, in Wrentham, Massachusetts. I wrote to them immediately, and received an invitation to come to Wrentham for a visit. My roommate Ellen was horrified. She found the letter cold and assured me that I wasn't the type for such a life. I was not fazed by this judgment, and set up a date when I would be free to come.

I drove down to Massachusetts as soon as I could, knocked on the door, and walked into the vestibule. There was a "turn" in the wall, and in answer to my ring I heard a voice saying *"Benedicamus Domino"* from the other side. I quickly recovered my tongue, and said who I was and why I had come. I was sent into a "parlor" and a sister came to speak with me. I was on one side of a double grille, and she was on the other side. She asked me if I was inquiring or applying to enter. I quickly said, "I'm inquiring!!" We talked for a little while, and then I heard a bell ringing and the sister said that was the warning bell for the Office of None. She told me how to get to the church on the guest side. I followed her directions. There were heavy curtains and a grille between the guest chapel and the sisters' area. The Divine Office was sung all in Latin. Nothing happened except one simple but important thing: the sudden, clear response in my heart, "This is it!!" When I saw the sister who had interviewed me again, I told her, "I'm applying!" She urged me to keep in touch and pray over it. I finished my visit and went back north. Both of my parents were very unhappy about my choice, but I wasn't going to be swayed by my great love for them. Jesus comes first, and He is calling me, I said to myself. The only one who supported me was Helen. She seemed to understand my need to undertake a way of life that seemed such a mystery to others.

I was invited to return to Wrentham to meet the Reverend Mother, Abbess Angela Norton. I did that in the early summer of 1955. She asked me whether I wanted to be a "lay sister" or a "choir sister," explaining what the words meant. This hadn't crossed my mind before, but I said I'd like choir because I love music and love to sing. She didn't think much of my singing but she did accept me, and we set a date I would come to enter:

October 7. I was very happy with that, and went back home rejoicing with a long list of things to bring with me, including an ankle-length black woolen dress, black shoes of a special kind with a small heel, a beret, veiling material, work outfits, blankets, etc. All of this was collected. I enjoyed my last summer with my family and friends. Then we all received a blow we hadn't imagined. My Dad was found to have lung cancer. He went for surgery in a large hospital near Hanover, New Hampshire. After the surgery we were informed that the doctors could do nothing to take out the diseased tissue because of its location. I called Mother Angela and told her what our situation was. She thought I should still come to enter on the set date. My mother was very upset about that and went to complain to Fr. John Doherty, who came to me to ask if I would mind if he went down to see Mother Angela to explain the situation. I agreed, with the stipulation that he make it clear that putting off my entrance was not my idea. Father went to see Mother Angela, and she agreed to put off my entrance because of the circumstances.

The doctors didn't have the equipment to give Dad radiation, so they suggested he go to Boston. He was taken to the Massachusetts General Hospital, where the equipment was available. My mother and I went after him in our car, saw him settled in, and went to stay with relatives who lived in the area. Dad died on the night of October 16–17. He looked so peaceful the nurse thought he was asleep and didn't want to wake him, not realizing what had happened. His body was brought to our family grave site in Vermont. I realized Mother needed me for at least some months, since Helen was going back to college and she would be left all alone. Anne had finished her time with the Waves and had been with us, but had a job and was living elsewhere. To cut a long story short, I stayed with Mother until June of 1956. The day came to say goodbye. Mother was brave but sad. My dog stood behind the screen door cocking her head right and left, trying to figure out what was happening. Helen and I climbed into the car, and drove away, stopping at the cemetery for me to pray a goodbye to Daddy and Agnes. We arrived in time for lunch with cousins in the Boston area, and then went on to the monastery.

Mother Angela met me at a door into the cloister. I said goodbye to Helen, and she started the return trip to New Hampshire. Mother Angela had me change into my postulant clothes. She asked me if there was a name I would like to have. I said I hadn't really thought about it, but that I would like Agnes although they probably already had an Agnes. She said that Agnes was what they were going to call me, after Mother Agnes of Glencairn, Mount Saint Mary's mother house.* It was clear that was the name the Lord wanted for me too!

I'm going to stop here because the contents of this book will give you a good idea of what life at Mt. St. Mary's was and is like. I went through joy and troubles, growing to love my new sisters and our way of life, and sharing with them Jesus' hidden presence. I had a good novitiate with about twelve postulants and novices and a novice mistress who helped us through the ups and downs that are the natural part of learning how to listen in order to live the monastic life. I received the novice's habit on December 28, 1956, made first vows in 1958, and solemn vows on December 8, 1961. I have had various jobs over the years, including making vestments, milking cows, helping in the sacristy, working in the art department, haying in season, etc. I worked in the shoe shop for a number of years. I became Mother Angela's secretary, which was something of a joke since I type with two fingers, but she kept me on anyway. I was appointed prioress (second superior) about nine years before Mother Angela's death, which happened in January of 1986. The election of a new abbess took place on the feast of Saint Benedict's death, March 21, and the result was a shock to me: I was elected for six years. At the end of that period we had another election, and I was reelected for an "indefinite" term. After twenty-two years in office, I resigned as abbess on May 5, 2008, and two weeks later we elected Mother Maureen McCabe. I am now happily a simple nun, sharing in the work and prayer and life of the community.

---

* In Cistercian language, a "mother house" is a monastery responsible for the foundation of a new monastery or "daughter house."

Since this little book deals with my experience of community life, more biography isn't needed, and as for the future, it hasn't happened yet. God bless you!

Summer 2012

SELECTED POEMS

Night Places

There are keys for locking up
day places after Compline.
Night places are always open,
never locked,
but best in the cock watches.
Business is out of bounds in the free night.
Concerns, petty or weighty, sleep
on the other side of the bolted door,
and all the chatterings of day's demands
are stilled.
Night's speech is elementary:
silences,
the bubbling forth of waters
from the bottom of the well of being.
Darkness makes cells with no walls
in which we are solitary together
in the free night.
This is the home of Advent,
open like faith for God's coming . . .
this simple Sabbath in which we dwell,
remembered, living, awaiting
another kind of dawn.

I Who Come

Must you have flames for Pentecost?
May I not come to you
    as soft as summer rain?
Folly to miss My gentler gift,
    expecting wind and earthquake.
Do not limit My language to fire.
Listen to me in the raindrops.
Flames were for yesterday,
    and mighty winds to cry My coming.
Today I pour out My Spirit as water.
I come to sing over you in tongues of rain,
    renewing you with My love.
I am transparent with charity.
Is my speech less eloquent
    if tongues are undivided
    and clear as tears?

Ladders

Between truck loads,
when bales stopped
coming up
our chain of arms,
the empty elevator
clattered on
with rhythmic thumps,
but we were still.

A sequence of sisters
up on stacked hay,
we sat, or leaned,
collapsed or stood,
waiting, like ladder rungs,
pointed — O shadowy rafters,
watching barn swallows swoop
through long shafts of light
alive with dust.

A mist of dust —
most humble of all stuff,
dried up,
dead matter sloughed, small bits
of earth's detritus
sticks to my sweat
tickles my lungs
grates in my eyes.
It is good for nothing. . . .

Nothing?
By a shift of focus
see, it magnifies
the light, intensifies
twin rays by dancing,
bouncing brilliance

from its swirling surfaces.
See it show forth on us
light's effect:
a lively double ramp
that almost might
be climbed
to windows, to
the open sky. . . .

I look again,
and ponder parables
until more hay arrives,
and puts an end
to visions.

Wise Play

The last raindrops
enliven the surface
of the pool, the rock pool
in the heart of the garden
at the center of the monastery.
Its tension broken,
the water's surface explodes
in little flashes,
leaping to meet
the tear-shaped kamikazes
of the home-bound rain.
This is not war, but peace;
not sadness, but excess of joy.
It is the overspill of welcome
of water returning to its own.
The celebration goes on
under the surface
where the drops, dying
to difference, beget energy,
jostling the solid, stolid rocks.

No, not stolid. Rocks dance, too,
a dance that began, that continues
deep in the pressures below,
miles below the pool, where rocks
are cracked, crumbled, melted;
kneaded like bread, juiced like grapes,
pulsed down veins to the core.
There at the center, rock is as water,
one river of living fire,
the inner side of light, magma
seething in ferment of new birth.
Now it cannot be restrained. Fiercely
spurting sudden upward artery,

it vents in volcano under the sea.
The depths boil, and fathoms above
the distant waves dance livelier
to the sun, returning. New creation
is a moving circle, out and in,
dynamic play of form and power.

Dynamic gift of love, the dance
goes on. Tomorrow rain may fall again
into our garden pool,
which now serenely mirrors
the white Montmartre Christ
and the wide, blue sky.

A Different Perspective

The blue glass jar
fell from the sill,
shattering; releasing
the lovely-prisoned air.

A stunned millifraction
it stood there, freed
air, shaped like
the inside of a jar.

Molecules danced across
the gone boundaries,
filling the room
with undetectable fragrance.

The perfume of freedom
spread outside, riding
the winds to the four
corners of the world.

Lost, did you say?
No, it's all here
bonded to atmosphere,
uniting the earth.

Mourn the unbroken?
Weep for a prison!
Our values are too
small, too sensual.

Shard of blue glass
lovely on the sill
now holds open-curved
the utterly vast.

Prologue to Day

Isaiah is a room
for Advent reading
with doors to north and south and west
and many eastern windows.
Shadows still shroud,
but windows to the dawn
are glad with light.
If vistas are obscure
still, sunrise caught in rumpled glass
makes brilliant dazzle patterns!
Glory splashes Isaiah.
On his window sill
the Christmas cactus glows.
Outside, in clarity,
where morning has already come,
though birds are silent for December,
John sings.

Advent Meditation
(O Antiphons for the last 7 days of Advent)

O Word of God,
one Word without end,
singing through all creation,
You are never static,
never stopped as with a final syllable,
yet perfect and complete
like a circle.
Heaven and earth are full of your glory
for all things
reflect You, echo You, point to You,
crying "O!" for the ultimate Advent.

You *are* Wisdom
reaching from end to end,
not in linear infinity
but as ends meet to form a circle.
Come, O Word containing all wisdom!
"I came forth from the Father
and I return to the Father."
The ends meet in the Father.
There is nowhere
where the ends do not meet
mightily and sweetly.
Teach us faith in Your wisdom!

O Word from the flaming bush,
You are word of the Law,
the Law of Love.
Omnipotent Word, the great I Am,
You become Adonai, strong warrior,
with mission to save,
You choose *kenosis,* choose
mute outstretched arms on the cross,
hanging, naked,
as emptied circle: zero, nothing . . .
nothing but love.
Teach us to trust
in such saving love!

O Root of Jesse, root and flower,
You are Adam
not of new clay, but of our race:
this people, *this* family,
this grandfather;
yet before Abraham came to be,
You Are.
Alpha and Omega,
You stand for an ensign of humanity
gathering up mankind in Yourself.
You are The Man, speaking man's words
from God's Heart.
Teach us to listen heedfully!

O Key of David,
You Yourself are the key to everything;
solution to the puzzle of life,
key to the vision of the Father.
"No one comes to the Father
except through Me."
O is the shape of all things
waiting for You,
the waiting locks of the universe,
the eager human mind.
You open and no one closes.
You close and no one opens.
Close us to sin and death,
open us to fullness of life!
O is nothing, and You are Everything
turning the tumblers of the mind.
"No one knows the Father
except the Son,
and those to whom the Son
chooses to reveal Him."
O, to be so chosen!

A circle of Light
before whom darkness flees,
O Rising Dawn,
You are not like the sun,
The sun is like *You!*
You are true Light of the world.
You come to give life,
to reveal the Father,
to cast fire on the earth,
on tinder of prisoned hearts
to burn them free. . . .
Burn us with Your truth,
to set love free in us, O Lord,
to live in Your light!

O King of the Gentiles,
Royal Word,
You are the Great Link,
making both one.
You are infinite Richness,
Desire of all!
O come and rule all in us,
You, who are essentially King!
Teach us to be one in You!

O Emmanuel,
God-with-Us,
hidden, soon to be
unveiled, a Child
to fill the void,
to curl, as throned, within
the ready curve of Virgin's arm,
we wait, round-eyed,
dilated by our hope
to see Your face!
Word yet wordless,
hearts are listening
for announcement
by your baby wail, "I'm here!"—
God's love your meaning.
O make us simple when we bend at Mary's knee;
the broken circle of our lives, a bow to You!
Let us, then, be with You,
God-with-Us,
silent in our gaping need
for You to fill with saving
when and as You will.

O Christ,
Word of the Father,
hear the groan of all creation:
You are meant to be All in all!
O come, be All in us!

O, in all the tongues of humanity,
O—sung, spoken, cried, whispered—
O, soundless in shapes:
circles and spheres,
in the fragment of curves.
O! O! O! We long for You!
How long, O Lord?
When will we see You face to Face?
O! Will it be
Tomorrow?

No Joy Unnoticed

He sent his snow
as white as wool
to coat the tablet of our garth,
and then the sun
to turn it crystalline.

The bird he sent
down winter air
knew not the why of impulse
prompting the descent,
or what its feet imprinted there.

Cuneiform,
I saw it tracked,
over the sleeping flower bed
double three forward,
double one back.

In chiseled pairs—
filigreed art—
the living claws had pressed
a pattern there,
a hop apart.

Hieroglyphics
of hunger eased?
Or maybe record
of a moment seized
for people-watching?

Two wings, one flight.
The bird is gone.
Behind, the sculptured
echo lingers on,
and my delight.

Tracks in the garth
are sown, and grace.
In Sower's Heart the noticed joy
is harvest
from my face.

Listen

Prayer is a calling.
It is also a response to a calling.
Prayer is a listening.

Prayer is a dwelling.
Prayer is a presence.

Prayer is a lamp,
aflame with Jesus.
Prayer is a watch
in the night.

Prayer is a language.
Prayer is a silence.
Prayer is a seeking
and also a finding.

Prayer is an openness
inundated with wonder.
Prayer is a wonder
inundated with God.
Prayer is an astonishment.

Prayer is a chanted melody with words
and wordless singing in the heart.

Prayer is a duty,
cherished as privilege.
Prayer is a life
for the glory of God.

Prayer is a bread,
kneaded with the agony of the world
for the miracle of Christing.

Prayer is sacrifice,
Liturgy, Mass.

Prayer is a love in the heart of the Church.

Prayer is a healing of breaches,
a building of bridges,
a breaking of barriers.

Prayer is a service,
A power, world-girdling.
Strong with compassion,
prayer is a way.

Prayer is a life
for the life
of the Church.

Prayer is
a spring of psalms
in the thirsty noon.
Prayer is a living water
welling within us . . .
a water that murmurs,
"Come to the Father."

Prayer is a desire.

Prayer is a plowing of ground
ordained to fruitfulness.
Prayer is a sprouting of seed.

Prayer is a hunger, and food for hunger.
Prayer is a giving . . . also a gift.
Prayer is a wholeness.

Prayer is a depth
in the smile of eyes.
Prayer is a sharing
of burdens.

Prayer is a bond
as strong as Christ.
Prayer is a communion.

Prayer is a discipline
leading to freedom.
Prayer is a simple yes to God.

Prayer is a burning desert
where the steel of love
is tempered in white-hot furnaces.
Prayer is a searing by the truth,
but also a delighting in the truth.
Prayer is a joy.

Prayer is anguish, agony, dying . . .
shattered by unthinkable resurrections.
Prayer is a paradox.

Prayer is a stillness.
Prayer is a peace.
Prayer is a rhythm
of quiet breathing,
and beat of a heart.

Prayer is a consecration,
commitment, oblation.
Prayer is a nothingness
filled with the All.

Prayer is a smashing of jars
and a spilling of nard.
Prayer is a life
for the life of the world.

Still Point

A desert to cross
with sheep not mine—
a daily search for pasture
for wells, for springs.
And then God's mountain
for desire's reach:
bare up-thrust rock
barren of bushes but one
and that on fire!
On fire yet seemingly
not burnt I must see
more closely, hear
with inner ear a Voice
not heard before,
calling from heart of flames
my name! Yes!
Here I am!

Response first manifest
in mind's swift leap
of wonder, now become
a stillness. A command:
"Put off your thoughts.
This ground is holy!"
His Name—I AM.

A space for utter silence
there where a bush
is leafed in fire—

A time for flocks again
but flocks in flame
to love-seared sight!

The inner ears
that held the Name
will ever catch the echo
in a world of desert
where the searcher
must remain a nomad
until the end of time
opens the gates.

The Heart of the Question

Each of us knew
His call meant love
from the beginning.
When it became a question
demanding an answer
each said yes
in wondering, small voice;
though we did not really understand
the question.
His love too large, too free.
How can narrow hearts say yes
to a question without boundaries?
a question leading God knows where?
But yes it had to be.

Designs of His heart . . .
Yes, God knows where.
We thought we chose
But it was He
who led us to this place—
this for each
and each for this—
(His plans are intricate)
knowing our poverty,
He knew we couldn't
grow our way alone.
Others appear in the question—
others too, intrinsic part of answer—
a community of others
living together as one in Christ.

Nor is the question static, disembodied.
United under one
who holds the place of Christ

we joy to make a whole
by invitation and response;
direction and glad following—
the sacrament of the Divine question.
We are given a way to walk,
a challenge, a promise.
We travel on a journey of return,
together;
saying with Mary,
"Be it done to me,"
with Jesus
"Abba! Behold I come to do Your will!"

Our *yes* expands
And little by little we learn
to be big enough to be little;
to be secure enough to let go;
free enough to enjoy like a child,
to laugh, to trust, to wonder,
to become a child again
for the sake of the Kingdom.

The darkness of the question
is lit by sudden gleams
in the deep silences of the night,
as we listen to One who speaks
in silence,
in a new way every day.
We know the glory of His voice
in the joy of a silent heart.

The answer grows stronger in us
as we pray in union
with the prayer of the Church;

rebuilding the ancient bridges of the psalms
with timbers from our daily lives,
uniting times, places, minds.
Words are not enough.
We find *yes* impels us
to be praise incarnate,
eucharist in the Eucharist,
Godwardness of heart
spread all over the day,
spilled into the night,
until it runs even through dreams.
We live to be music to God,
part of a great voice that is one—
Christ's voice.

We come to know all things
from the inside,
hearing God's call to them
in our own,
understanding that they all point to Christ,
that He is their meaning.
With the seasons we move
through newness, growth,
fruitfulness, rest.
We die and are born again—
to a new level of the question.

The question burns, for love is fire.
We have to be assayed by truth
to come to purity of heart:
all that deviates falls away charred—
pretense and dear illusion,
the wrong answers we use to hide behind—
self's barriers must crumble.

We must be stripped to heartwood,
arrow-straight—pure gift,
a little all, affecting all,
which draws all toward wholeness.

Living as one in Christ,
we become a sign of unity in the Church,
and even more,
for in some microscopic way,
by the centripetal force of love,
the day is hastened when all will be one
as Jesus asks.

He teaches us to grow in living unity
in which we are not lost
but find our true selves.
He lets us find dynamic unity
more than sum total of all parts.
He draws us to swim upstream
in the mystery,
to find community flowing from its Sources:
His inner life of love
with Father and Holy Spirit.

The heart of the question
is question of one Heart—
Christ's.
The answer too, at last commensurate.
Redemptive love is His alone
and yet He makes it ours
to channel to each other,
widening us in the torrent.